## Introduction

*All you need to know about retirement planning* has been written as a reference book to give you advice on how to plan your retirement. Karl and Tristan Hartey understand the importance of making sure you have the correct plans in place to allow you to enjoy your retirement.

# Chapters

# Chapter one
## What are you planning for?

**When was the last time you wrote down your goals?**
**More importantly, when was the last time you revisited them?**
A new year can be seen as a fresh start and a marker to look forward to what you want to accomplish – personally, professionally and hopefully financially. Maybe you have already thought, 'This is the year I must start contributing more to my retirement,' or, 'This is the year I'm finally going to say goodbye to credit card debt.'

Regardless of what life stage you are in, the start of a new year is the perfect time to take stock of your financial plans and to ensure that you have the right goals and strategies in place to achieve them. Remember the old adage, 'People don't plan to fail, but they do fail to plan.'

## Tangible and realistic

You are likely to have short-term, mid-term and long-term personal financial goals. The key to ultimately achieving them is to set tangible and realistic goals and to follow them, and tracking your progress is essential to obtain your financial goals this year and beyond.

If you are married, you and your spouse or registered civil partner should both share the same financial goals. Otherwise, achieving them is almost impossible. Developing your financial plans together and reviewing your progress together to make sure both of you are contributing to the same goals is essential.

## Financial goals

Determining what short-term, mid-term and long-term personal financial goals you have is the first step. This could be building an emergency savings fund, buying a new or second property, accumulating funds for your children's schooling and further education, or building an investment portfolio and saving for your retirement.

Once you and your spouse have agreed on your target objectives, the next step is to determine a good estimate for how much money you'll need for each of them. To obtain a clear understanding of the amounts involved and the options available to achieve these requires professional financial advice.

## Decisions, decisions

For example, if you are saving for higher education for your children, what percentage do you want to pay? Also, do you want to pay for a state school or a private school education? Retirement savings needs depend greatly on the lifestyle you plan to lead once you are retired, as well as when you plan to retire.

## Estimated average

There are a number of factors you need to consider before deciding on what kind of approach is most suitable for you. These include the purpose of the investment, the length of time your money can be tied up for and your attitude to risk.

It's also important to prioritise each of your personal financial goals in order of importance and then determine how long you have to save or invest for each of them. Retirement could be many years away, but your short-term goals could be in a year or two. You then need to estimate how much interest or capital gains you'll expect to see where you are saving or investing your money. While capital gains are never guaranteed, you can use an estimated average for these purposes to arrive at target figures.

A mistake some people also make is that once their plans are in place, they forget to look at them again or not as frequently as they should. It's important to continue to refine your plans going forward and use these reviews to allocate any other amounts you may receive, for example, from bonuses or inheritances. Realistically, will you really be able to accomplish everything? Probably not. You never know what could come up, but 'you'll always miss the shots you don't take'. Think of your financial goals like that.

# Chapter two
## Assessing current and forecasted wealth

To be in a position to navigate the financial aspects of your unique life's journey, you need to regularly track your progress towards key goals such as paying off your mortgage, buying a second home, building a retirement fund or setting up an Inheritance Tax trust.
Clarity over your goals is key, as are your objectives and motivations. The process of cash flow modelling illustrates what might happen to your finances in the future and enables you to plan to ensure that you make the most of your money to achieve your financial objectives.

**Current and forecasted wealth**
Cash flow modelling shows your current position relative to your preferred position and your goals by assessing your current and forecasted wealth, along with income inflows and expenditure outflows to create a picture of your finances, now and in the future. This detailed picture of your assets includes investments, debts,

income and expenditure, which are projected forward year by year using calculated rates of growth, income, inflation, wage rises and interest rates.

In order to implement a detailed plan that outlines how to deliver your financial future, communication is vital. The process and planning are only as good and as comprehensive as the information you provide.

## Right asset allocation mix

Cash flow modelling can determine the best course of action for your particular situation, the right asset allocation mix, and the growth rate you require is calculated to meet your investment objectives. This rate is then cross-referenced with your attitude to risk to ensure your expectations are realistic and compatible with the asset allocation needed to achieve the necessary growth rate.

Where cash flow modelling becomes particularly useful is the analysis of different scenarios based on decisions you may make – this could be lifestyle choices or perhaps investment decisions. By matching your present and expected future liabilities with your income and capital, recommendations can be made to ensure that don't run out of money throughout your life.

## Ensure you remain on track

A snapshot in time is taken of your finances. The calculated rates of growth, income, tax and so on that are used to form the basis of any cash flow modelling exercise will always be assumptions. Therefore, regular reviews and reassessments are required to ensure you remain on track.

Nearly all decisions are based on what is contained within the cash flow: from how much to save and spend, to how funds should be invested to achieve the required return, so there is a lot that needs to be managed.

**Implementing a lifetime cash flow plan can enable you to:**

- Produce a clear and detailed summary of your financial arrangements
- Define your family's version of the 'good life' and begin working towards it
- Work towards achieving and maintaining financial independence
- Ensure adequate provision is made for the financial consequences of the death or disablement of you or your partner
- Plan to minimise your tax liabilities
- Produce an analysis of your personal expenditure planning assumptions, balancing your cash inflows and your desired cash outflows
- Estimate future cash flow on realistic assumptions
- Develop an investment strategy for your capital and surplus income in accordance with risk/reward, flexibility and accessibility with which you are comfortable
- Become aware of the tax issues that are likely to arise on your own death and that of your partner.

**Make the right financial decisions**
With every financial corner you turn, it is important to 'run through the numbers', which will help you make the right financial decisions. It is important to be specific. For example, it is not enough to say, 'I want to have enough to retire comfortably.' You need to think realistically about how much you will need – the more specific you are, the easier it will be to come up with a plan to achieve your goals.

If your needs are not accurately established, then the cash flow will not be seen as personal, and therefore you are unlikely to perceive value in it.

**Small tweaks or something significant**
Some years, there may not be any change, or just small tweaks. However, in other years, there may be something significant; either

way, you will need to ensure things are up to date to keep your own peace of mind knowing your plans are still on track.

Cash flow modelling helps you stay in control of your financial future by giving a more holistic planning approach and clearer picture of the consequences of change on an ongoing basis. It also helps to give an idea of when certain key decisions should be made, such as retiring early or downsizing a property.

# Chapter three
## Looking ahead to your retirement years

From stopping work altogether to a slow and gradual reduction of commitments – retirement means different things to different people. Making sure you can sustain the level of income you need as you move away from full-time employment or your business interests is key to a long and happy retirement.

### Increased complexity
While pension rule changes in recent years have increased their flexibility, they have also increased the complexity. But pensions still offer a very favorable tax status, and there are now more ways than ever to generate income from pension assets when you retire: from buying an annuity to taking a lump sum or making regular withdrawals while continuing to invest.

In April 2015, the Government introduced the most radical changes to pensions in almost a hundred years. The pension freedoms (announced by the previous Chancellor, George Osborne, in Budget 2014 and introduced on 6 April 2015) now mean that instead of being required to buy an annuity with your money purchase pension pot, if you're aged 55 and over you have more flexibility to take your money how you wish. Generally, 25% of the pot is tax-free, and the remainder is subject to Income Tax at your current rate.

## Financial structure
A critical aspect of retirement planning is how you structure your financial affairs to make sure you have sufficient money if and when you stop working. Making sure you have enough money in retirement to enable you to spend your time the way you want to and do those things you always intended is at the heart of planning for your retirement.

We are all living longer – the State Pension Age has steadily increased and pensions legislation is ever-changing. It makes sense to reassess your situation and to ensure you have in place a flexible retirement strategy that will enable you to enjoy yourself and still look after your family.

## Other considerations
Retirement planning also involves more than just thinking about pensions. Individual Savings Accounts (ISAs), general investments, property, National Savings and cash deposits can all play a part in a retirement plan too.

The pension changes mean that we'll be increasingly in charge of our pensions, both while we're building up our retirement pot and when we start to draw an income. It's therefore more important than ever to plan our retirement saving from an early age.

## Getting started
If you're not saving for retirement, it's time to get started. The sooner you start, the more time your money has to grow. Make saving for your retirement in 2019 one of your top priorities. Remember, it's never too early or too late to start saving.

But remember that if you already have a retirement strategy in place, it pays to be prepared as retirement nears. Around two years before you want to stop working is a good time to start thinking about your retirement options and the choices you'll need to make. You should obtain professional financial advice because these are decisions that can shape your income for the rest of your life.

# Chapter four
## Pension power

From stopping work altogether to a slow and gradual reduction of commitments – retirement means different things to different people. Making sure you can sustain the level of income you need as you move away from full-time employment or your business interests is key to a long and happy retirement.

Pensions are a highly tax-efficient form of saving, and if possible, you should take full advantage of funding your pension contributions to the maximum allowable. You receive tax relief on contributions that you pay into your pension. Tax relief means some of your money that would have gone to the Government as tax goes into your pension instead. You can put as much as you want into your pension, but there are annual and lifetime limits on how much tax relief you get on your pension contributions.

## Tax relief on your annual pension contributions

If you're a UK taxpayer, in the tax year 2019/20 the standard rule is that you'll get tax relief on pension contributions of up to 100% of your earnings or a £40,000 annual allowance, whichever is lower:

- For example, if you earn £20,000 but put £25,000 into your pension pot (perhaps by topping up earnings with some savings), you'll only get tax relief on £20,000.
- Similarly, if you earn £60,000 and want to put that amount in your pension scheme in a single year, you'll normally only get tax relief on £40,000.

## Subject to Income Tax

Any contributions you make over this limit will be subject to Income Tax at the highest rate you pay. However, you can carry forward unused allowances from the previous three years, as long as you were a member of a pension scheme during those years.

But there is an exception to this standard rule. If you have a defined contribution pension, the annual allowance reduces to £4,000 in some situations.

From 6 April 2016, the £40,000 annual allowance reduced if you have an income of over £150,000, including pension contributions.

## Money Purchase Annual Allowance (MPAA)

In the tax year 2019/20, if you start to take money from your defined contribution pension, this can trigger a lower annual allowance of £4,000 (the MPAA). That means you'll only receive tax relief on pension contributions of up to 100% of your earnings or £4,000, whichever is the lower.

Whether the lower £4,000 annual allowance applies depends on how you access your pension pot, and there are some complicated rules around this.

This announcement will affect taxpayers (employees and self-employed) who have withdrawn amounts from their pension fund and then want to top the fund up again. The £10,000 limit was introduced in April 2015 and reduced to £4,000 from April 2017.

The Chancellor, Philip Hammond, said the decision was taken 'to prevent inappropriate double tax relief,' and the Government would consult on further details for the plans. In a consultation released alongside the Autumn Statement, the Government says: 'The Government believes that an allowance of £4,000 is fair and reasonable and should allow people who need to access their pension savings to rebuild them if they subsequently have opportunity to do so. 'Importantly, however, it limits the extent to which pension savings can be recycled

to take advantage of tax relief, which is not within the spirit of the pension tax system. The Government does not consider that earners aged 55 plus should be able to enjoy double pension tax relief i.e. relief on recycled pension savings.'
This change will impact on those individuals who may have needed to withdraw funds unexpectedly and then want to top them up when their circumstances change.

**The main situations when you'll trigger the MPAA are typically:**

- If you start to take ad-hoc lump sums from your pension pot
- If you put your pension pot money into an income drawdown fund and start to take income

**You will not trigger it if you take:**

- A tax-free cash lump sum and buy an annuity (an insurance product that gives you a guaranteed income for life)
- A tax-free cash lump sum and put your pension pot into an income drawdown product but don't take any income from it

You can't carry over any unused MPAA to another tax year.

**Defined contribution pensions**
The existing lower annual allowance of £4,000 only applies to contributions to defined contribution pensions. So, if you also have a defined benefit pension (this pays a retirement income based on your final salary and how long you have worked for your employer and

includes final salary and career average pension schemes), you can still receive tax relief on up to £40,000 of contributions a year.

For example, if you earn £20,000 a year and you contribute £8,000 to your defined contribution pension for the tax year 2019/20, you'll receive tax relief on these contributions, plus you can still receive tax relief on up to £12,000 of contributions to your defined benefit pension.

If you earn £50,000 a year and you contribute £12,000 to your defined contribution pension for the tax year 2019/20, you'll receive tax relief on just £4,000 (and the other £8,000 will be subject to Income Tax). In addition, you can contribute up to £36,000 to your defined benefit pension and claim tax relief on this.

## Tax relief if you're a non-taxpayer
If you are not earning enough to pay Income Tax, you can still receive tax relief on pension contributions up to a maximum of £3,600 a year or 100% of earnings, whichever is greater, subject to your annual allowance. For example, if you have relevant income below £3,600, the maximum you can pay in is £2,880, and the Government will top up your contribution to make it £3,600.

# Chapter five
## Take your pension to the max

A lifetime allowance puts a limit on the value of pension benefits that you can receive without having to pay a tax charge. The lifetime allowance is £1,055,000 for the tax year 2019/20. Any amount above this is subject to a tax charge of 25% if paid as pension or 55% if paid as a lump sum.

It applies to the total of all the pensions you have, including the value of pensions promised through any defined benefit schemes you belong to, but excluding your State Pension.

From 6 April 2018, the standard lifetime allowance will be indexed annually in line with the Consumer Prices Index (CPI).

## Charges if you exceed the lifetime allowance

If the cumulative value of the payouts from your pension pots, including the value of the payouts from any defined benefit schemes, exceeds the lifetime allowance, there will be tax on the excess – called the 'lifetime allowance charge'.

The way the charge applies depends on whether you receive the money from your pension as a lump sum or as part of regular retirement income.

## Lump sums

Any amount over your lifetime allowance that you take as a lump sum is taxed at 55%. Your pension scheme administrator should deduct the tax and pay it over to HM Revenue & Customs (HMRC), paying the balance to you.

## Regular retirement income

Any amount over your lifetime allowance that you take as a regular retirement income – for instance, by buying an annuity – attracts a lifetime allowance charge of 25%. This is on top of any tax payable on the income in the usual way.

For defined contribution pension schemes, your pension scheme administrator should pay the 25% tax to HMRC out of your pension pot, leaving you with the remaining 75% to use towards your retirement income.

## Lifetime allowance charge and Income Tax combined

For example, suppose someone who pays tax at the higher rate had expected to get £1,000 a year as income but the 25% lifetime allowance reduced this to £750 a year. After Income Tax at 40%, the person would be left with £450 a year. This means the lifetime allowance charge and Income Tax combined have reduced the income by 55% – the same as the lifetime allowance charge had the benefits been taken as a lump sum instead of income.

For defined benefit pension schemes, your pension scheme may decide to pay the tax on your behalf and recover it from you by reducing your pension.

If you wish to avoid the lifetime allowance charge, it's important to monitor the value of your pensions, and especially the value of changes to any defined benefit pensions as these can be surprisingly large.

The 'annual allowance' is a limit on the amount that can be contributed to your pension each year, while still receiving tax relief. It's based on your earnings for the year and is capped at £40,000, which still remains unchanged following the Autumn Statement 2016.

# Chapter six
## Misplaced pensions pots

It's not always easy to keep track of a pension, especially if you've been in more than one scheme or have changed employer throughout your career. The extent to which pension policies are being forgotten has been revealed in research from Aviva. A survey of almost ten thousand people who hold a pension has revealed that just under one in eight (13%) admitted they have at least one pension that they had forgotten about [1]. This is equal to more than 2.5 million pension policies currently sitting in the back of people's minds [2].

**Have you received a refund?**
If you left an employer before April 1975, it's likely you will have received a refund of your pension contributions. If you didn't pay into

the scheme, you probably won't be entitled to anything, unless you were in the scheme for at least 15 to 20 years.

If you left the employer between April 1975 and April 1988, you will have a pension, provided you were over age 26 and had completed five years in the scheme. If not, you will almost certainly have had a refund of your pension contributions and have no further rights.
If you left the employer after 1988, you will be entitled to a pension, as long as you completed two years' service. If you left the pension scheme with fewer than two years' service, you probably received a refund of your contributions at the time you left.

## Misplaced or forgotten?
Among those with a forgotten pension, the majority believe they have misplaced one pot (77%), although 17% think they have forgotten about two and 6% have forgotten three or more.

According to government figures, there is an estimated £400 million in unclaimed pension savings [3]. At the same time, almost three in five (59%) UK adults are worried about not having enough money to last them in retirement [4].

## Annual statement
Most pension schemes of which you've been a member must send you a statement each year. These statements include an estimate of the retirement income that the pension pot may generate when you reach retirement.

If you're no longer receiving these statements – perhaps because of changes of address – then to track down the pension there are three bodies to contact: the pension provider, your former employer if it was a workplace pension, or the Pension Tracing Service (an online service available to help you find contact information).

## Boost to retirement
Although tracking down a lost pension can provide a valuable boost to retirement income, those who delay could receive a smaller amount than expected. Forgotten pensions may have been subject to charges and not invested in the best way suited to the

policyholder, making it worth less than it would have been if it was actively managed.

The research revealed the lack of engagement around pensions. More than a quarter of savers (28%) admitted to never reviewing their retirement savings, while almost a fifth (19%) of those with a pension said they review it less than once every five years [5].

## Fund choices

Since the introduction of auto-enrolment, the number of pension savers who are unaware of their fund choices or have never reviewed them has risen to almost 1.5 million people or 15% of private sector employees, up from 9% at the start of 2013[6].

It's also important to be aware of the potential consequences of having a number of different pension pots with small amounts of money in each. It's likely that there will still be charges taken out of those pots for their management and administration, and that can have implications if you are no longer contributing into them.

## Source data:

[1] YouGov survey of 9,910 people in the UK (January–December 2015) who hold a pension carried out on behalf of Friends Life, now part of the Aviva group
[2] ABI Key Facts 2015 says there are 20.8m individual pension policies in force. 13% of 20.8m = 2.7m
[3] DWP: https://www.gov.uk/government/news/new-pension-tracing-service-website-launched
[4] Research conducted for Aviva
by Censuswide, with 2002 General Consumers aged 18+ in GB between 30 September and 5 October 2016. The survey was conducted from a random sample of UK adults.
[5] YouGov survey of 9,498 people in the UK carried out on behalf of Friends Life, now part of the Aviva Group
[6] Aviva's latest Working Lives Report and analysis of data from the Office for National Statistics (ONS).

# Chapter seven
## Building a more secure financial future

To make the most of your investment opportunities, it's your goals that count, so keep them firmly in mind when you make financial decisions. It's important to take a consistent, long-term strategy to build a more secure financial future through steady purchases of well-diversified investments.

**Main types of investment**
There are four main types of investments, known as 'asset classes'. Each asset class has different characteristics and advantages and disadvantages for investors.

## Cash

This involves putting your money into a savings account, with a bank, building society or credit union. Your money may not hold its spending power if inflation is higher than the interest rate. Cash is the most basic of all investment forms. Saving money into a deposit account with a bank, building society or credit union is considered cash saving. Cash can be used to save for immediate needs or as a parking place in between investing in other assets.

## Why have cash savings?

If you need instant access to your money or are saving for the near future, cash could be a good option. You earn interest on cash. How much you earn varies from one account to another. You can save in cash without paying tax on the interest by saving in a Cash Individual Savings Account (ISA).

## What are the risks?

The amount you invest will not go down in actual terms, but you may lose spending power if interest rates you receive don't keep up with inflation rates while you are saving. In other words, the nominal value of your savings will stay the same, but the real value could fall.

Cash deposits are guaranteed against the failure of a bank, building society or credit union from 1 January 2017 to the value of £85,000 per person by the Financial Services Compensation Scheme.

## Bonds

A bond is a loan to a government or company. In return for the loan, you receive interest and the amount you invested back at an agreed future date. Bonds are issued by governments and companies as a way for them to borrow money. In return, lenders get paid interest and the full value of their money back at a specified date, called the 'redemption date'.

As an example:
The market price of a bond will rise as interest rates are expected to fall. Bonds have a fixed interest rate. Imagine you hold a bond with a fixed interest rate of 5% whilst general interest rates fall from 4% to

2%. Your bond would be a lot more attractive when general interest rates are 2%; therefore, its price on the market rises.

## What are bonds?

Bonds issued by the UK Government are called 'gilts'. You can buy these directly at the Post Office or the Government Debt Management Office.

Bonds issued by companies are called 'corporate bonds'. They are bought and sold on the stock market. Their price will go up and down, which means that if you decide to sell before the agreed redemption date, you may get more or less than the price you originally paid.
The interest you receive from your bond will be specified before you buy. While the end value and annual interest payments are normally fixed amounts, in some cases (such as with UK Government index-linked gilts) they may be related to a price index.

Index-linked bonds ensure your money keeps in line with inflation, but at times of low inflation a fixed rate bond could provide higher returns.

## What are the risks of investing in bonds?

There is still the risk that the issuer may be unable to fulfil its promise to return your money on the redemption date. This could mean that you lose some or all of your initial investment. To help you manage this risk, bonds are rated by credit rating agencies. The rating on a bond is a good guide on how capable the issuer is in paying back their debt i.e. how likely you are to get your money back when the term of the bond ends.

## Shares

You can invest in a company by buying shares. In return, you may get a proportion of any profit the company makes (depending on how many shares you hold). Shareholders are entitled to have a say on the way the company operates, including voting at company general meetings.

Companies issue shares, often referred to as 'equities', as a way of raising money from outside investors. In return, the investor may receive a portion of the company's profit, called a 'dividend'. Investors receive a dividend for each share they own. Shareholders are in effect the owners of a company.

## Why invest in shares?
- Historically, shares have been one of the highest performing asset classes over long periods
- Dividends are normally paid annually or biannually
- Dividend payments have usually risen over time. But if a company suffers a loss, dividend payments can decline or even stop

## What are the risks?
The value of your shares is dependent on a number of things including the performance of the company and the wider economic outlook. The value can go up and down over time. It is sensible to invest in shares only if you can afford to put money away for a period of years. The fluctuating nature of the value of shares means you do not want to be forced to withdraw your money when share prices are low, as you may get back less than your original investment.

## Property
Becoming a landlord is a well-known way to invest in property. The aim is to get an income from the rent you charge and that the house or flat increases in value after expenses, so you make a profit if you sell it. Land and commercial buildings, such as shopping centres, are other forms of property investments.

## Why invest in property?
Property provides a relatively high and stable rental income with the possibility of making your money grow over time.

## What are the risks of investing in property?
Buying and selling buildings can take a long time, and if you invest in property you might not be able to withdraw your cash as quickly as you would wish. Investing in property via a fund generally means it is easier to get access to your cash when you need it.

However, providing this level of access can mean lower returns. The value of properties fluctuates over time, so there is a potential that you could lose money.

You can invest in property by buying a property on a buy-to-let basis. However, the cost and complexity of owning and managing an individual property is high.

**There are two ways to invest in property indirectly:**

- Invest in shares of companies that own or develop properties
- Invest in a property fund which gives you exposure to a range of assets. These may include property company shares or commercial property such as offices, shopping centres and warehousing.

| Asset class | Main advantages | Main risks |
| --- | --- | --- |
| Cash | Relatively secure | May lose value if the interest rate doesn't keep up with inflation. |
| Bonds | Regular income | The bond issuer is sometimes unable to repay in full. |
| Shares | Regular income and opportunity to grow over time. | Share prices can go up and down. A fall in share price will reduce the value of your investment. |
| Property | Stable and regular income, potential to grow over time. | Property prices can fall, reducing the value of your investment. Property transactions take a long time, so your money may be tied up for longer than you want it to be. |

# Chapter eight
## Managing investment risk

One of the most effective ways to manage investment risk is to spread your money across a range of assets that, historically, have tended to perform differently in the same circumstances. This is called 'diversification' – reducing the risk of your portfolio by choosing a mix of investments.

In the most general sense, it can be summed up with this phrase: 'Don't put all of your eggs in one basket'. While that sentiment certainly captures the essence of the issue, it provides little guidance on the practical implications of the role of diversification plays in a portfolio.

Under normal market conditions, diversification is an effective way to reduce risk. If you hold just one investment and it performs badly, you could lose all of your money. If you hold a diversified portfolio with a variety of different investments, it's much less likely that all of your investments will perform badly at the same time. The profits you earn on the investments that perform well offset the losses on those that perform poorly.

**Minimising risk**
While it cannot guarantee against losses, diversifying your portfolio effectively – holding a blend of assets to help you navigate the volatility of markets – is vital to achieving your long-term financial goals whilst minimising risk.

Although you can diversify within one asset class – for instance, by holding shares (or equities) in several companies that operate in different sectors – this will fail to insulate you from systemic risks, such as international stock market volatility.

**Diversification**
As well as investing across asset classes, you can diversify by spreading your investments within asset classes. For instance, corporate bonds and government bonds can offer very different propositions, with the former tending to offer higher possible returns but with a higher risk of defaults, or bond repayments not being met by the issuer.

Similarly, the risk and return profiles of shares in younger companies in growth sectors like technology, for example, contrast with those of established, dividend-paying companies.

**Portfolio insulation**
Effective diversification is likely to also allocate investments across different countries and regions in order to help insulate your portfolio from local market crises or downturns. Markets around the world tend to perform differently day to day, reflecting short-term sentiment and long-term trends.

There is, however, the added danger of currency risk when investing in different countries, as the value of international currencies relative to each other changes all the time. Diversifying across assets valued in different currencies or investing in so-called 'hedged' assets that look to minimise the impact from currency swings, should reduce the weakness of any one currency significantly decreasing the total value of your portfolio.

## Individual investors

Achieving effective diversification across and within asset classes, regions and currencies can be difficult and typically beyond the means of individual investors. For this reason, some people choose to invest in professionally managed funds that package up several assets rather than building their own portfolio of individual investments.

Individual funds often focus on one asset class, and sometimes even one region, and therefore typically only offer limited diversification on their own. By investing in several funds, which between them cover a breadth of underlying assets, investors can create a more effectively diversified portfolio.

## Multi-asset fund

One alternative is to invest in a multi-asset fund, which will hold a blend of different types of assets designed to offer immediate diversification with one single investment. Broadly speaking, their aim is to offer investors the prospect of less volatile returns by not relying on the fortunes of just one asset class.

Multi-asset funds are not all the same, however. Some aim for higher returns in exchange for assuming higher risk in their investments, while others are more defensive, and some focus on delivering an income rather than capital growth. Each fund will have its own objective and risk-return profile, and these will be reflected in the allocation of its investments – for instance, whether the fund is weighted more towards bonds or equities.

## Long-term view

Stock markets can be unpredictable. They move frequently – and sometimes sharply – in both directions. It is important to take a long-term view (typically ten years or more) and remember your reasons for investing in the first place.

Be prepared to view the occasional downturns simply as part of a long-term investment strategy and stay focused on your goal.
Historically, the longer you stay invested, the smaller the likelihood you will lose money and the greater the chance you will make money. Of course, it's worth remembering that past performance is not a guide to what might happen in the future, and the value of your investments can go down as well as up.

## Time to grow

Give your money as much time as possible to grow – at least ten years is best. You'll also benefit from 'compounding', which is when the interest or income on your original capital begins to earn and grow too. There will be times of market volatility. Market falls are a natural feature of stock market investing. During these times, it is possible that emotions overcome sound investment decisions – it is best to stay focused on your long-term goals.

## Market timing

Resist the temptation to change your portfolio in response to short-term market movement. 'Timing' the markets seldom works in practice and can make it too easy to miss out on any gains. The golden rule to investing is allowing your investments sufficient time to achieve their potential.

Warren Buffett, the American investor and philanthropist, puts it very succinctly: 'Our favourite holding period is forever.' Over the long term, investors do experience market falls which happen periodically. Generally, the wrong thing to do when markets fall by a reasonable margin is to panic and sell out of the market – this just means you have taken the loss. It's important to remember why you're invested in the first place and make sure that rationale hasn't changed.

# Chapter nine
## Generating income

One of the most effective ways to manage investment risk is to spread your money across a range of assets that, historically, have tended to perform differently in the same circumstances. This is called 'diversification' – reducing the risk of your portfolio by choosing a mix of investments.

Nobody knows quite what the future holds. The good news is that advances in medicine and healthier lifestyles have led to an increase in the average life expectancy of both males and females.

The downside is we now have to find ways of funding a longer retirement and longevity. But low interest rates and bond yields – the traditional sources of income – aren't sufficient to sustain a proper living.

## Varying income
Changing life plans and priorities will mean we encounter varying income needs and goals throughout our life, and, when investing, certain innate behavioral traits will influence our decision-making.

With interest rates at historic lows, investors need to consider diversifying across asset classes and internationally to obtain the desired levels of income. Equities, emerging market (EM) debt and high-yield corporate bonds could help generate a real yield, albeit at some risk to capital.

## Attractive income
Weak domestic growth and unorthodox monetary policies have pushed down core bond yields and kept bank account cash rates low. Investors are likely to find it difficult to generate a 'decent' real income from many sources previously considered reliable and 'safe'. Dividends from equity holdings provide a stable and consistent source of income.

## Alternative income
Emerging market debt provides a high yield. Many EM economies have lower government debt levels than G7 countries, but offer higher yields, providing attractive opportunities for investors.

The investable universe of EM debt has grown significantly in recent years. Active management is key to seeking out the attractive opportunities and avoiding those that are most at risk.

## Higher-yielding debt

Given the yields available from both the US and European high-yield sector, and the current low level of defaults, some investors may prefer high yield over investment-grade bonds.

While there are concerns over the high-yield energy sector, the US high-yield market is highly diversified by sector and includes access to many other quality names. Most companies can still comfortably afford their interest payments.

## Investment implications

In this current environment, investors need to think beyond traditional sources of income to beat inflation, and if appropriate consider multi-asset investing. This may mean taking on more risk, but a well-diversified portfolio can help reduce volatility.

Equity dividends can be an important source of income and have historically been very stable. Also, think about EM and high-yield debt as part of a portfolio, as they can offer attractive yields relative to core bonds.

# Chapter ten
## Tax relief and pensions

With careful planning and professional financial advice, it is possible to take preventative action to either reduce your beneficiaries' potential Inheritance Tax bill or mitigate it out altogether.

Tax relief means some of your money that would have gone to the Government as tax goes into your pension instead. You can put as much as you want into your pension, but there are annual and lifetime limits on how much tax relief you get on your pension contributions.

## Tax relief on your annual pension contributions
If you're a UK taxpayer, the standard rule is that you'll receive tax relief on pension contributions of up to 100% of your earnings or a £40,000 annual allowance, whichever is lower.

For example, if you earn £20,000 but put £25,000 into your pension pot (perhaps by topping up earnings with some savings), you'll only get tax relief on £20,000. Similarly, if you earn £60,000 and want to put that amount in your pension scheme in a single year, you'll normally only get tax relief on £40,000.

Any contributions you make over this limit will be subject to Income Tax at the highest rate you pay. However, you can carry forward unused allowances from the previous three years, as long as you were a member of a pension scheme during those years.

There is an exception to this standard rule however. If you have a defined contribution pension, and you start to draw money from it, the annual allowance reduces to £4,000 in some situations.

From 6 April 2016, the £40,000 annual allowance was reduced if you have an income of over £150,000, including pension contributions.

## The Money Purchase Annual Allowance (MPAA)
In the tax year 2019/20, if you start to take money from your defined contribution pension, this can trigger a lower annual allowance of £4,000 (down from £10,000 with effect from 6 April 2017). This is known as the 'Money Purchase Annual Allowance' (MPAA).

That means you'll only receive tax relief on pension contributions of up to 100% of your earnings or £4,000, whichever is the lower.

Whether the lower £4,000 annual allowance applies depends on how you access your pension pot, and there are some complicated rules around this.

**The main situations when you'll trigger the MPAA are:**

- If you start to take ad-hoc lump sums from your pension pot
- If you put your pension pot money into an income drawdown fund and start to take income

**The MPAA will not be triggered if you take:**

- A tax-free cash lump sum and buy an annuity (an insurance product that gives you a guaranteed income for life)
- A tax-free cash lump sum and put your pension pot into an income drawdown product but don't take any income from it

You can't carry over any unused MPAA to another tax year.

The lower annual allowance of £4,000 only applies to contributions to defined contribution pensions and not defined benefit pension schemes.

**Tax relief if you're a non-taxpayer**
If you're not earning enough to pay Income Tax, you'll still qualify to have tax relief added to your contributions up to a certain amount. The maximum you can pay is £2,880 a year or 100% of your earnings – subject to your annual allowance.

Tax relief is added to your contribution, so if you pay £2,880, a total of £3,600 a year will be paid into your pension scheme, even if you earn less than this.

**How much can you build up in your pension?**
A lifetime allowance puts a top limit on the value of pension benefits that you can receive without having to pay a tax charge.

The 2019/20. lifetime allowance is £1,055,000 million for the tax year. Any amount above this is subject to a tax charge of 25% if paid as pension or 55% if paid as a lump sum.

**Workplace pensions, automatic enrolment and tax relief**
Since October 2012, a system is being gradually phased in requiring employers to automatically enroll all eligible workers into a workplace pension.

It requires a minimum total contribution, made up of the employer's contribution, the worker's contribution and the tax relief.

# Chapter eleven
## Lifetime allowance

The lifetime allowance is a limit on the value of payouts from your pension schemes – whether lump sums or retirement income – that can be made without triggering an extra tax charge. The lifetime allowance for most people is £1,055,000 in the tax year 2019/20.

It applies to the total of all the pensions you have, including the value of pensions promised through any defined benefit schemes you belong to, but excluding your State Pension.

From 6 April 2018, the Government intends to index the standard lifetime allowance annually in line with the Consumer Prices Index (CPI).

Working out if this applies to you Every time a payout from your pension schemes starts, its value is compared against your remaining lifetime allowance to see if there is additional tax to pay.
You can work out whether you are likely to be affected by adding up the expected value of your payouts.
**You work out the value of pensions differently depending on the type of scheme you are in:**

- For defined contribution pension schemes, including all personal pensions, the value of your benefits will be the value of your pension pot used to fund your retirement income and any lump sum.

- For defined benefit pension schemes, you calculate the total value by multiplying your expected annual pension by 20. In addition, you need to add to this the amount of any tax- free cash lump sum if it is additional to the pension. In many schemes, you would only get a lump sum by giving up some pension, in which case the value of the full pension captures the full value of your payouts. So, you  are likely to be affected by the lifetime allowance in 2019/20 if you are on track for a final salary pension (with no separate lump sum) of more than £50,000 a year, or a salary-related pension over £37,500 plus the   maximum tax-free cash lump sum.

- Note that certain tax-free lump sum benefits paid out to your survivors if you die before age 75 also use up lifetime allowance.

- Whenever you start taking money from your pension, a statement from your scheme should tell you how much of your lifetime allowance you are using up.

- Whether or not you take money from your pension, a check will be made once you reach the age of 75 against any unused funds or undrawn entitlements.

**Charges if you exceed the lifetime allowance**
If the cumulative value of the payouts from your pension pots, including the value of the payouts from any defined benefit schemes, exceeds the lifetime allowance, there will be tax on the excess – called the 'lifetime allowance charge'.
The way the charge applies depends on whether you receive the money from your pension as a lump sum or as part of regular retirement income.

**Lump sums**
Any amount over your lifetime allowance that you take as a lump sum is taxed at 55%. Your pension scheme administrator should deduct the tax and pay it over to HM Revenue & Customs (HMRC), paying the balance to you.

**Income**
Any amount over your lifetime allowance that you take as a regular retirement income – for instance, by buying an annuity – attracts a lifetime allowance charge of 25%. This is on top of any tax payable on the income in the usual way.

For defined contribution pension schemes, your pension scheme administrator should pay the 25% tax to HMRC out of your pension pot, leaving you with the remaining 75% to use towards your retirement income.

For example, suppose someone who pays tax at the higher rate had expected to get £1,000 a year as income, but the 25% lifetime allowance charge reduced this to £750 a year. After Income Tax at 40%, the person would be left with £450 a year.

This means the lifetime allowance charge and Income Tax combined have reduced the income by 55% – the same as the lifetime allowance charge had the benefits been taken as a lump sum instead of income.

For defined benefit pension schemes, your pension scheme might decide to pay the tax on your behalf and recover it from you by reducing your pension.

If you wish to avoid the lifetime allowance charge, it's important to monitor the value of your pensions, and especially the value of changes to any defined benefit pensions, as these can be surprisingly large.
You might also wish to consider applying for protection if your pension savings is expected to exceed the lifetime allowance threshold.

# Chapter twelve
## State pension

The State Pension changed on 6 April 2016. If you reached State Pension age on or after that date, you'll get the new State Pension under the new rules.

The new State Pension is designed to be simpler than the old system, but there are some complicated changeover arrangements which you need to know about if you've already made contributions under the old system.

## Already receiving a State Pension
If you were already receiving a State Pension before 6 April 2016, you'll continue to receive your State Pension under the old rules.
However, if you're a woman born before 6 April 1953 or a man born before 6 April 1951, your State Pension will be paid under the old system. Even if you deferred your State Pension to a date after 6 April 2016, it will still be calculated under the old system.

## State Pension under the old system
Women born on or after 6 April 1953 or men born on or after 6 April 1951 will receive the new State Pension. If someone has already started to build up a State Pension under the old system, this will be converted into an amount under the new State Pension.

If they hadn't built up any State Pension by 6 April 2016, their State Pension will be completely calculated under the new rules.

## Changes to the State Pension
The earnings-related part of the old system which applied to employed people called the 'Additional State Pension' is abolished.

The new State Pension is based on your National Insurance (NI) record alone. For the current tax year, the new State Pension is £164.35 per week. However, someone may receive more than this if they have built up entitlement to Additional State Pension under the old system – or less than this if they were 'contracted out' of the Additional State Pension. To be eligible for the full £164.35 per week, someone will need 35 years' NI record.

## 'Starting amount' under the new State Pension
The new State Pension is calculated from your NI record as at 6 April 2016, converted into a 'starting amount' under the new State Pension. This won't be lower than the amount you would have received under the old system.

Under the old system, if you were employed (rather than self-employed), you paid Class 1 National Insurance which entitled you to the Basic State Pension and an Additional State Pension. The Additional State Pension was based on your earnings as well as the National Insurance contributions you had made or been credited with.

## Substantial entitlement to Additional State Pension

If you had built up substantial entitlement to Additional State Pension, this might mean that you have already earned a pension under the old system which is worth more than £164.35 a week. If this applies to you, you will get the full new State Pension amount, and you'll also keep any amount above this as a 'protected payment' which will increase by inflation. However, you won't be able to build up any more State Pension after April 2016.

If your starting amount is equal to the full new State Pension, you'll receive the full new State Pension amount. You won't be able to build up any more State Pension after April 2016.

If your starting amount is lower than the full new State Pension, this might be because you were 'contracted out' of the Additional State Pension. You can continue to build up your State Pension to the maximum (currently £164.35 per week) up until you reach State Pension age.
You can do this even if you already have 35 years of NI contributions or credits.

## Less than 35 years of NI

- To receive the full amount, you'll need to have 35 years' worth of NI contributions or credits (known as 'qualifying years') during your working life. These don't have to be consecutive years
- If you have less than 35 years of NI contributions or credits, you'll receive an amount based on the number of years you have paid or been credited with NI
- If you have less than ten years, you won't normally qualify for any State Pension

- However, the ten-year minimum qualifying period does not apply to certain women who paid married women and widow's reduced-rate National Insurance contributions
- If you have gained qualifying years in the European Economic Area, Switzerland or certain bilateral countries which has a social security agreement with the UK, these can be used towards achieving the minimum qualifying period. However, the actual UK State Pension award will normally be based on just the UK qualifying years

## Deferring the new State Pension

You'll still be able to defer taking your State Pension. For each year you defer, you'll receive just under a 5.8% increase in your State Pension (compared to 10.4% under the old system). You cannot take the deferred amount as a lump sum.

The new State Pension is normally based on your own NI contributions alone, but you may be able to have your State Pension worked out using different rules that could give you a higher rate if you chose to pay married women and widow's reduced-rate NI contributions (sometimes called the 'married woman's stamp').

## Not enough NI record to qualify for State Pension

If you have not yet reached State Pension Age but are worried that you might not have enough NI record to qualify for State Pension (or to receive the maximum amount), you can make Class 3 National Insurance contributions. These contributions are voluntary and allow people to fill gaps in their record to improve their basic State Pension entitlement.

You should regularly request a State Pension statement so that you can see how much State Pension you've built up so far.

# Chapter thirteen
## Defined contribution pension schemes

With a defined contribution pension, you build up a pot of money that you can then use to provide an income in retirement. Unlike defined benefit schemes, which promise a specific income, the income you might get from a defined contribution scheme depends on factors including the amount you pay in, the fund's investment performance and the choices you make at retirement.

Defined contribution pensions build up a pension pot using your contributions and your employer's contributions (if applicable) plus investment returns and tax relief. If you're a member of the scheme through your workplace, then your employer usually deducts your contributions from your salary before it is taxed. If you've set the scheme up for yourself, you arrange the contributions yourself.

The fund is usually invested in stocks and shares, along with other investments, with the aim of growing it over the years before you retire. You can usually choose from a range of funds to invest in. Remember, though, that the value of investments can go up or down.

**The size of your pension pot and amount of income you receive when you retire will depend on:**

- How much you pay into your pot
- How long you save for
- How much your employer pays in (if a workplace pension)
- How well your investments have performed
- What charges have been taken out of your pot by your pension provider
- How much you take as a cash lump sum
- The choices you make when you retire
- Annuity rates at the time you retire – if you choose the annuity route.

When you retire, your pension provider will usually offer you a retirement income (an annuity) based on your pot size. However, you don't have to take this, and it isn't your only option

# Chapter fourteen
## Defined benefit pension schemes

A defined benefit pension scheme is one where the amount paid to you is set using a formula based on by how many years you've worked for your employer and the salary you've earned rather than the value of your investments. If you work or have worked for a large employer or in the public sector, you may have a defined benefit pension.

Defined benefit pensions pay out a secure income for life which increases each year. They also usually pay a pension to your spouse or registered civil partner and/or your dependants when you die. The pension income they pay is based on:

- The number of years you've been a member of the scheme – known as 'pensionable service'

- Your pensionable earnings – this could be your salary at retirement (known as 'final salary'), salary averaged over a career ('career average'), or some other formula
- The proportion of those earnings you receive as a pension for each year of membership – this is called the 'accrual rate', and some commonly used rates are 1/60th or 1/80th of your pensionable earnings for each year of pensionable service.

These schemes are run by trustees who look after the interests of the scheme's members. Your employer contributes to the scheme and is responsible for ensuring there is enough money at the time you retire to pay your pension income.

Check your latest pension statement to get an idea of how much your pension income may be. If you haven't got one, ask your pension administrator to send you one. Statements vary from one scheme to another, but they usually show your pension based on your current salary, how long you've been in the scheme and what your pension might be if you stay in the scheme until the scheme's normal retirement age.

If you've left the scheme, you'll still receive a statement every year showing how much your pension is worth. In most cases, this pension will increase by a set amount each year up until retirement age. Contact your pension administrator if you're not receiving your annual statement.

**The more you take, the lower your income**
When you take your pension, you can usually choose to take up to 25% of the value of your pension as a tax-free lump sum. With most schemes, your pension income is reduced if you take this tax-free cash. The more you take, the lower your income. But some schemes, particularly public sector pension schemes, pay a tax-free lump sum automatically and in addition to the pension income.

Make sure you understand whether the pension shown on your statement is the amount you'll get before or after taking a tax-free lump sum. Also, don't forget that your actual pension income will be taxable.

Most defined benefit schemes have a normal retirement age of 65. This is usually the age at which your employer stops paying contributions to your pension and when your pension starts to be paid.

If your scheme allows, you may be able to take your pension earlier (from the age of 55), but this can reduce the amount you get quite considerably. It's possible to take your pension without retiring.

Again, depending on your scheme, you may be able to defer taking your pension, and this might mean you get a higher income when you do take it. Check with your scheme for details.

### Yearly increases

Once your pension starts to be paid, it will increase each year by a set amount – your scheme rules will tell you by how much. It will continue to be paid for life. When you die, a pension may continue to be paid to your spouse, registered civil partner and/or dependants. This is usually a fixed percentage (for example, 50%) of your pension income at the date of your death.

You may be able to take your whole pension as a cash lump sum. If you do this, up to 25% of the sum will be tax-free, and the rest will be subject to Income Tax. You can usually do this from age 55 or earlier if you're seriously ill.

# Chapter fifteen
## Personal pensions

A personal pension is a type of defined contribution pension. You choose the provider and make arrangements for your contributions to be paid. If you haven't got a workplace pension, getting a personal pension could be a good way of saving for retirement.

Your pension provider will claim tax relief at the basic rate and add it to your pension pot. If you're a higher rate taxpayer, you'll need to claim the additional rebate through your tax return. You also choose where you want your contributions to be invested from a range of funds offered by your provider.

Your pension pot builds up in line with the contributions you make, investment returns and tax relief. The fund is usually invested in stocks and shares, along with other investments, with the aim of growing the fund over the years before you retire. You can usually choose from a range of funds to invest in.

**When you retire, the size of your pension pot when you retire will depend on:**

- How much you pay into your pension pot
- How long you save for
- How much, if anything, your employer pays in
- How well your investments have performed
- What charges have been taken out of your pot by your pension provider.

Following changes introduced in April 2015, you now have more choice and flexibility than ever before over how and when you can take money from your pension pot.

# Chapter sixteen
## Using your pension pot

Under the pension freedoms rules introduced in April 2015, once you reach the age of 55, you can now take your entire pension pot as cash in one go if you wish. However, if you do this, you could end up with a large tax Income Tax bill and run out of money in retirement. It's essential to obtain professional advice before you make any major decisions about how to access your pension pot.

### Closing your pension pot
If you want to take your entire pension pot as cash, you simply close your pension pot and withdraw it all. The first 25% is tax-free, and the remaining 75% is taxed at your highest Income Tax rate, calculated by adding it to the rest of your income.

This approach won't provide a regular income for you – or for your spouse or any other dependant after you die. Three quarters of the amount you withdraw is taxable income, so there's a possibility that your tax rate could increase when the money is added to your other income. Once you have exercised this option, you can't change your mind.

**Tax-efficient approaches to consider before taking your pension**
There are likely to be a number of alternative tax-efficient approaches you should consider first before taking your pension. Withdrawing a large cash sum could reduce any entitlement you have to benefits now, or as you grow older – for example, to help with long-term care needs. Also, cashing in your pension to clear debts, buy a holiday or indulge in a big-ticket item will reduce the money you will have to live on in retirement – and you could end up with a large tax bill.

Depending on how much your pension pot is, when it's added to your other income it might increase your tax rate. Your pension scheme or provider will pay the cash through a payslip and take off tax in advance – called 'PAYE' (Pay As You Earn). This means you might pay too much Income Tax and have to claim the money back – or you might owe more tax if you have other sources of income.

**Exceeding the lifetime allowance**
Extra tax charges or restrictions might apply if your pension savings exceed the lifetime allowance (currently £1,055,000 2019/20), or if you have reached age 75 and have less lifetime allowance available than the value of the pension pot you want to cash in.

If the value of the pension pot you cash in is £10,000 or more, once you have taken the cash, the annual amount of defined contribution pension savings on which you can get tax relief is reduced from £40,000 (the Money Purchase Annual Allowance or MPAA) to £4,000 (MPAA). If you want to carry on building up your pension pot, this option might not be suitable.

If you die, any remaining cash or investments from the money that came from your pension pot will count as part of your estate for Inheritance Tax purposes. Whereas any part of your pot not used would not normally be liable.

# Chapter seventeen
## Taking your pension

Under the new flexible pension freedoms rules, you can now mix and match various options, using different parts of one pension pot or using separate or combined pots.

**Leave your pension pot untouched**
You might be able to delay taking your pension until a later date. Your pot then continues to grow tax-free, potentially providing more income once you access it.

It's important to check with your pension scheme or provider whether there are any restrictions or charges for changing your retirement date, and the process and deadline for telling them. Also check that you won't lose any income guarantees – for example, a guaranteed annuity rate (GAR) – by delaying your retirement date. The value of pension pots can rise or fall. Remember to review where your pot is invested as you get closer to the time you want to retire and arrange to move it to less risky funds if necessary. If you want to delay taking your pot but your scheme or provider doesn't have this option, obtain advice and shop around before moving your pension.

The longer you delay, the higher your potential retirement income. However, this could affect your future tax and your entitlement to benefits as you grow older, for example, long-term care costs.

You could instead delay taking some of your pension. For example, you might be able to arrange to retire gradually, or change to working part-time or flexibly and then draw part of your pension. If you want your pot to remain invested after the age of 75, you'll need to check with your pension scheme or provider that they will allow this. If not, you might need to transfer to another scheme or provider who will.

- **If you die before age 75:** your untouched pension pots can pass tax free to any nominated beneficiary. The money will continue to grow tax- free as long as it stays invested, and, provided they take it within two years of your death, the beneficiary can take it as a tax-free lump sum or as tax- free income. If they take it later, the pay tax on it.
- **If you die after 75:** if your nominated beneficiary takes the money as income or as a lump sum payment, they'll pay tax at their marginal rate. This means that the money will be added to their income and taxed in the normal way

If the total value of all your pension savings when you die exceeds the lifetime allowance (currently £1 million), further tax charges will be payable by the beneficiary.

## Guaranteeing a regular retirement income for life
You can choose to take up to 25% of your pension pot as a one-off tax-free lump sum, then convert the rest into a taxable income for life called an 'annuity'. A lifetime annuity is a type of retirement income product that you buy with some or all of your pension pot. It guarantees a regular retirement income for life. You can also choose to provide an income for life for a dependent or other beneficiary after you die.

Lifetime annuity options and features vary – what is suitable for you will depend on your personal circumstances, your life expectancy and your attitude to risk. You can normally choose to take up to 25% of your pension pot – or of the amount you're allocating to buy an annuity – as a tax-free lump sum.

This retirement income from an annuity is taxed as normal income. Typically, the older you are when you take out an annuity, the higher the income (annuity rate) you'll get.

**Two types of lifetime annuity to choose from:**

- **Basic lifetime annuities -** where you set your income in advance
- **Investment-linked annuities** - where your income rises and falls in line with investment performance but will never fall below a guaranteed minimum.

Basic lifetime annuities offer a range of income options designed to match different personal circumstances and attitude to risk.

**Decide whether you want:**

- One that provides an income for life for you only – a single life annuity, or one that also provides an income for life for a dependant or other nominated beneficiary after you die (called a 'joint life annuity')

- Payments to continue to a nominated beneficiary for a set number of years (for example, ten years) from the time the annuity starts in case you die unexpectedly early – called a
- 'guarantee period'

- 'Value protection' – less commonly used, but designed to pay your nominated beneficiary the value of the pot used to buy the annuity less income already paid out when you die.

Your choices affect how much income you can receive. Also where you expect to live when you retire may affect how much income you get. If you have a medical condition, are overweight or smoke, you might be able to get a higher income by opting for an 'enhanced' or 'impaired life' annuity.

## Investment-linked annuities
Investment-linked annuities also pay you an income for life, but the amount you get can fluctuate depending on how well the underlying investments perform. If the investments do well, they offer the chance of a higher income. However, you have to be comfortable with the risk that your income could fall if the investments don't do as well as expected. All investment-linked annuities guarantee a minimum income if the fund's performance is weak.

With investment-linked annuities, you can also opt for joint or single annuity, guarantee periods, value protection and higher rates if you have a short life expectancy due to poor health or lifestyle. However, not all providers will offer these options.

## Flexible retirement income – flexi-access drawdown
With flexi-access drawdown, when you come to take your pension, you reinvest your pot into funds designed to provide you with a regular retirement income. This income may vary depending on the fund's performance, and it isn't guaranteed for life. Unlike with a lifetime annuity, your income isn't guaranteed for life – so you need to manage your investments carefully.

You can normally choose to take up to 25% of your pension pot as a tax-free lump sum. You then move the rest into one or more funds that allow you to take a taxable income at times to suit you. Increasingly, many people are using it to take a regular income.

You choose funds to invest in that match your income objectives and attitude to risk and set the income you want. The income you receive might be adjusted periodically depending on the performance of your investments.

Once you've taken your tax-free lump sum, you can start taking the income right away or wait until a later date. You can also move your pension pot gradually into income drawdown. You can take up to a quarter of each amount you move from your pot tax-free and place the rest into income drawdown.

You can at any time use all or part of the funds in your income drawdown to buy an annuity or other type of retirement income product that might offer guarantees about growth and/or income.

Flexi-access drawdown is a complex product so it's important to obtain professional financial advice to discuss the options available. You need to carefully plan how much income you can afford to take under flexi-access drawdown, otherwise there's a risk you'll run out of money.

**This could happen if:**

- You live longer than you've planned for
- You take out too much in the early years
- Your investments don't perform as well as you expect and you don't adjust the amount you take accordingly.

If you choose flexi-access drawdown, it's important to regularly review your investments. Not all pension schemes or providers offer flexi-access drawdown. Even if yours does, it's important to compare what else is on the market, as charges, the choice of funds and flexibility might vary from one provider to another.

Any money you take from your pension pot using income drawdown will be added to your income for the year and taxed in the normal way. Large withdrawals could push you into a higher tax band, so bear this in mind when deciding how much to take and when.

If the value of all of your pension savings is above £1,055,000 when you access your pot (2019/20 tax year), further tax charges might apply.
If the value of your pension pot is £10,000 or more, once you start to take income, the amount of defined contribution pension savings which you can get tax relief on each year falls from £40,000 (the 'annual allowance') to £4,000 (the Money Purchase Annual Allowance or MPAA).

If you want to carry on building up your pension pot, this might influence when you start taking income. You can nominate who you'd like to receive any money left in your drawdown fund when you die.

- If you die before the age of 75, any money left in your drawdown fund passes tax-free to your nominated beneficiary whether they take it as a lump sum or as income. These payments must begin within two years of your death, or the beneficiary will have to pay Income Tax on them
- If you die after the age of 75 and your nominated beneficiary takes the money as income or lump sum, they will pay tax at their marginal rate. This means that any income or lump sum taken on or after this date will be added to their income and taxed in the normal way

**Combining your retirement options**
You don't have to choose one option when deciding how to access your pension – you can combine your options as appropriate and take cash and income at different times to suit your needs. You can also keep saving into a pension if you wish and get tax relief up to age 75.

**Which option or combination is right for you will depend on:**

- Your age and health
- When you stop or reduce your work
- Whether you have financial dependents
- Your income objectives and attitude to risk
- The size of your pension pot and other savings
- Whether your circumstances are likely to change in the future
- Any pension or other savings your spouse or partner has, if relevant

The choices you face when considering taking some or all of your pension pot are very complex, and you should obtain professional advice to assess your best option or combination of options.

# Chapter eighteen
## Buying an annuity

One way to use your pension pot is to buy an annuity. This gives you a regular retirement income, usually for the rest of your life. In most cases, this is a one-off, irreversible decision, so it's crucial to choose the right type and get the best deal you can.

Until recently, most people with a defined contribution pension (based on how much has been paid into their pension pot – also known as a 'money purchase pension') used their pot to buy an annuity.

However, you can now access and use your pension pot in any way you wish from age 55.

You don't have to buy an annuity from your pension provider; you can shop around on the open market to help ensure you get the best deal and options for you.

**Decide on the type of annuity you want**

Choosing an annuity is about more than getting the best value on the market. There are different annuity types (ones that pay an income for life – including basic lifetime annuities and investment-linked annuities – and 'fixed-term' annuities that pay an income for a set period).

Within these types, you have several options for how you want the income paid. It's important to choose the right annuity type and income options for your circumstances and pension pot.

**Higher income for poor health or lifestyle**

If you have a diagnosed medical condition or poor lifestyle, you could qualify for a higher retirement income from an 'enhanced annuity'. So don't hide your health problems or unhealthy lifestyle. It pays to tell your provider – and other providers when shopping around – if, for example, you're a smoker or have high blood pressure.

**Check what your pension provider is offering**

**At least six weeks before your retirement date, your provider will contact you with:**

- Details of the value of your pension pot
- An indication of the retirement income your pot would generate if you bought a basic lifetime annuity with it

It's important to check whether your agreement with your provider includes a guaranteed annuity rate (GAR). These can be very valuable as they can offer much better rates than those generally available. A GAR might come with restrictions but can lead to a significant boost to your retirement income.

The retirement income that your current provider offers you is your starting point for finding out if you can get a better rate elsewhere.

## Discuss your options

In most cases, choosing an annuity is a decision that will determine your income for the rest of your life, so it's extremely important to make the right choice.

You should discuss your findings with a professional financial adviser before choosing an annuity.

The law and tax rates may change in the future. These details are based on our understanding of tax law and HM Revenue & Customs' practice which is subject to change. The amount of tax you pay, and the value of any tax relief, will depend on your individual circumstances.

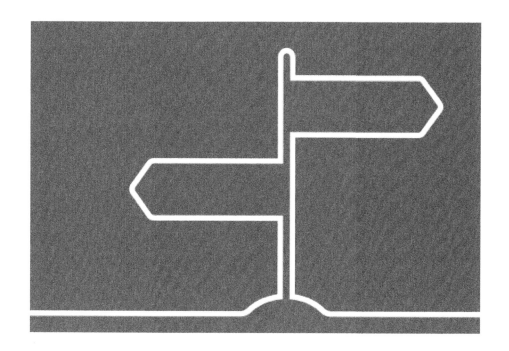

# Chapter nineteen
## Options at retirement

**WHEN AND HOW YOU USE YOUR PENSION**
Whether you plan to retire fully, reduce your hours gradually or to carry on working for longer, you can now tailor when and how you use your pension – and when you stop saving into it – to fit with your particular retirement plans.

Currently, the minimum age you can take any workplace or personal pension is age 55. You need to check with your scheme provider or insurance company to make sure the scheme will allow this. This is proposed to increase to age 57 by 2028.

From 2028 onwards, the proposal will be for the minimum pension age to increase in line with the State Pension age. This means there will be a 10-year gap between when you can take your own pensions and any State Pension you are eligible for.

There's a lot to consider when working out which option or combination will provide you and any beneficiaries with a reliable and tax-efficient income throughout your retirement.

## LEAVE YOUR PENSION POT UNTOUCHED

Once you reach the age of 55, you have the right to take as much of your pension fund as you like as cash – but that doesn't mean that you have to do so.

You may be able to delay taking your pension until a later date and may wish to leave your money where it is so that it still has the potential to grow – though your fund could also go down in value, of course. Equally, you might just want some time to consider all your options before deciding whether to take cash from your pension fund – and, if so, how much.

## USE YOUR POT TO BUY A GUARANTEED INCOME FOR LIFE – AN ANNUITY

You can choose to take up to a quarter (25%) of your pot as a one-off, tax-free lump sum, then convert the rest into a taxable income for life called an 'annuity'. There are different lifetime annuity options and features to choose from that affect how much income you would get. You can also choose to provide an income for life for a beneficiary after you die.

## USE YOUR POT TO PROVIDE A FLEXIBLE RETIREMENT INCOME – FLEXI-ACCESS DRAWDOWN

With this option, you take up to 25% (a quarter) of the pension pot that is being crystallised as a tax-free lump sum, then re-invest the rest into funds designed to provide you with a taxable income. You set the income you want, though this may be adjusted periodically depending on the performance of your investments (funds can be left alone to accrue if there is no immediate need for income). Unlike with a lifetime annuity, your income isn't guaranteed for life – so you need to manage your investments carefully.

Previously, there were government limits (known as 'Government Actuary's Department' or GAD limits) on how much income you could withdraw each year. This still applies to existing capped drawdown contracts where taxable income was being taken before 5 April 2015, providing the GAD limit is respected. These restrictions have been removed from 6 April 2015 for new flexi-access drawdown contracts.

## TAKE SMALL CASH SUMS FROM YOUR POT

If you're not sure how your income needs will change in the future, you may wish to take money from your defined contribution pension pots as and when you need it and leave the rest untouched. For each cash withdrawal, the first 25% (quarter) is tax-free, and the rest counts as taxable income. There may be charges each time you make a cash withdrawal and/or limits on how many withdrawals you can make each year.

# Chapter twenty
## Self-invested personal pension tax relief

Self-Invested Personal Pensions are one of the most tax-efficient ways of saving for retirement, and you can invest up to the annual allowance for tax relievable pension contributions (currently £40,000). As always, please bear in mind that tax relief will depend on your individual circumstances, and tax laws may change.

Effectively, whenever you contribute into a pension, the Government will give you tax relief calculated on your gross contributions based on the tax band you are in. Each tax band will get a different percentage, but it is a great boost to help you save for the future.

**Non-taxpayer:** You are entitled to 20% tax relief on £3,600. Therefore, you can contribute up to £2,880 into the SIPP.

**Basic-rate taxpayer:** You are entitled to 20% tax relief which is added to your pension pot.

**Higher-rate taxpayer:** You are entitled to 40% tax relief. Your SIPP will claim 20% and add this to your pension pot, but you will need to claim the further 20% through your tax return. The tax relief claimed from your tax return will not be automatically added to your SIPP.

**Additional-rate taxpayer:** You are entitled to 45% tax relief. Your SIPP will claim 20% and add this to your pension pot, but you will need to claim the further 25% through your tax return. Tax relief claimed from your tax return won't be automatically added to your SIPP.

**Non-taxpayer:** Even if you don't pay Income Tax, you're still entitled to tax relief at the same rate as a basic-rate taxpayer. The maximum you can claim relief on is £2,880 per tax year. If you contribute £2,880, you'll receive £720 tax relief, making the overall contribution into your SIPP £3,600.

EXAMPLES OF HOW TAX RELIEF IS APPLICABLE:

| | Total gross contribution in your SIPP | Your net contribution | Tax relief added to your pension pot | Tax relief from your tax return |
|---|---|---|---|---|
| Non-taxpayer | £3,600[1] | £2,880 | £720 | £0 |
| Basic-rate | £10,000 | £8,000 | £2,000 | £0 |
| Higher-rate | £10,000 | £8,000 | £2,000 | £2,000 |
| Additional | £10,000 | £8,000 | £2,000 | £2,500 |

# Chapter twenty-one
## Making self-invested personal pension investments

Self-Invested Personal Pensions are likely to be most suited to experienced investors who are comfortable choosing and managing investments themselves. You need to have the necessary skills to invest your own pension fund, and you must remember that the value of investments can fluctuate, so you could get back less than you invested.

Investing your retirement savings in a SIPP may not be for everyone, however. If you are uncertain as to what type of investment to invest in, then you should seek professional financial advice.

Although SIPPs offer greater flexibility than traditional pension schemes, they often have higher charges, and the time involved in research means they may be more suitable for experienced investors.

**Most SIPPs allow you to select from a range of assets, such as:**

- Unit trusts
- Investment trusts
- Government securities
- Insurance company funds
- Traded endowment policies
- Some National Savings and Investment products
- Deposit accounts with banks and building societies
- Commercial property (such as offices, shops or factory premises)
- Individual stocks and shares quoted on a recognised UK or overseas stock exchange.

These aren't all of the investment options that are available – different SIPP providers offer different investment options. Residential property can't be held directly in a SIPP with the tax advantages that usually accompany pension investments.

However, subject to some restrictions (including on personal use), residential property can be held in a SIPP through certain types of collective investments, such as real estate investment trusts, without losing the tax advantages.

A Self-Invested Personal Pension could be right for you if you are looking to build up a pension fund in a tax-efficient way and are prepared to commit to having your money tied up, normally until at least age 55. You need to understand that the value of your investments can fall as well as rise.

**Right for you if:**

- You want to build your pension pot tax-efficiently
- You're comfortable with the risk involved
- You're prepared to have the funds tied up for a long time – normally until you're at least 55

# Chapter twenty-two
## Self-invested personal pension contributions

Every year, you receive an allowance for making contributions into a Self-Invested Personal Pension. The Government sets this limit because your pension contributions are topped up with tax relief.
You can either pay lump sums into your SIPP, or you can make regular contributions – whichever suits you best.

Your employer or anyone else can also make contributions into your SIPP on your behalf. There's a limit on the amount of contributions you can make each year which attract tax relief. For most people, this is currently £40,000 per tax year, or 100% of your earnings – whichever is the lower. If you have enough income in the current year, you can increase contributions by any unused allowances for any of the last three tax years, provided that you belonged to a pension scheme at that time.

The usual £40,000 annual allowance is cut for people with annual earnings of more than £150,000. The allowance reduces by £1 for every £2 earned above £150,000, down to a minimum of £10,000 for those earning more than £210,000.

Non-taxpayers and children can currently also make pension contributions of up to £2,880 a year (making £3,600 with basic-rate tax relief).

**Your annual allowance will be reduced if:**

- You have drawn a taxable sum from a personal pension (in which case, the amount that you can pay into pensions and receive tax relief reduces to £4,000 per tax year), or 100% of your income – whichever is lower.

- If you earn over £110,000 and your income and pension contributions made on your behalf exceeds £150,000, your annual allowance will be tapered.

**More control over retirement investments**
If you have a UK registered pension scheme with another company, you can transfer its value into your pension fund. However, by transferring benefits from another pension provider into your Self-Invested Personal Pension, you may give up the right to guarantees over the kind of benefits, the amount you will receive and the level of increases that will be applied to your pension in the future.

Your existing pension provider may apply a penalty (or other reduction in the value of your benefits) if it is transferred. There is no guarantee that you will be able to match the benefits that you give up by transferring your pension.

If you are in any doubt about the benefit of transferring, you should seek professional advice before arranging the transfer.

## SIPP TRANSFER TO ANOTHER PENSION SCHEME

You can transfer the value of your SIPP to another UK registered pension scheme at any time. If you have started taking benefits from your SIPP, then you must transfer the whole of that part of your fund from which you are drawing benefits to your new scheme.

If you have uncrystallised funds, you can choose to transfer all, or only a part, of those uncrystallised funds to another pension scheme.

The transfer can be in the form of a cash payment, in which case you will have to sell all of the investments held under your SIPP before the transfer is completed, or you may be able to transfer them in their existing form (known as an 'in-specie transfer').

# Chapter twenty-three
## Lifetime allowance

There's also a maximum total amount that an individual can hold within all their pension funds without having to pay extra tax when you withdraw money from them. The lifetime allowance is a limit to the amount you can save in your Self-Invested Personal Pension or other pensions over your lifetime but excludes your State Pension. The allowance is currently £1 million – you will pay tax on any pension savings you make in excess of this. The excess is taxed at 25% (plus Income Tax) as income, or 55% as a lump sum.

Every time a payout from your pension schemes starts, its value is compared against your remaining lifetime allowance to see if there is additional tax to pay.

If the cumulative value of the payouts from your pension pots (including the value of the payouts from any defined benefit schemes) exceeds the lifetime allowance, there will be tax on the excess – called the 'lifetime allowance charge'.

The way the charge applies depends on whether you receive the money from your pension as a lump sum or as part of regular retirement income. Any amount over your lifetime allowance that you take as a lump sum is taxed at 55%.

From 6 April 2018, the Government intends to index the standard lifetime allowance annually in line with the Consumer Prices Index (CPI).

# Chapter twenty-four
## Pension carry forward

Pension allowances changed in 2016, and some people lost the Government's generous tax relief for pension contributions. Under pension carry forward rules introduced from 6 April 2011, you can make pension contributions above your annual allowance by carrying over unused allowance from the last three tax years.

You can carry forward the unused allowance, as long as you had a Self-Invested Personal Pension or other pension in place for each of the three years and your total contributions don't exceed your current earnings.

To use carry forward, you must make the maximum allowable contribution in the current tax year (£40,000 in 2019/20), and you can then use unused annual allowances from the three previous tax years, starting with the tax year three years ago.

Carry forward may be particularly useful if you are self-employed and your earnings change significantly each year, or if you're looking to make large pension contributions.

# Chapter twenty-five
## Pension freedoms

New rules about pensions came into effect on 6 April 2015, providing more choice for anyone who has a private or occupational money-purchase pension.

You can withdraw some or all of the money held in a money-purchase workplace or personal pension. This is providing you are over the age of 55 and have not already begun to draw on your pension or bought an annuity.

While you can still convert your pension into an annuity or invest it in a drawdown product, the new rules also enable you to withdraw the entirety of your pension, either as a lump sum or a series of withdrawals, subject to Income Tax above the first 25%.

However, bear in mind that if you withdraw too much from your pension in one go, it could move you into a higher Income Tax bracket.

From the age of 55:
- You can take a pension commencement lump sum, and/or;
- Start taking your pension income at any time, even if you are still working.

You may start taking a pension income before age 55 only if you are forced to take early retirement through ill health or you have a protected pension age.

Since April 2015 (subject to your pension scheme rules), for most pension investors aged at least 55, you will have total freedom over how you take an income or a lump sum from your pension.

- You can choose to take your entire pension pot as cash in one go – 25% tax-free and the rest taxed as income

- Take lump sums, as and when required, with 25% of each withdrawal tax-free and the rest taxed as income

- Take up to 25% tax-free and then a regular taxable income from the rest. Either via income drawdown (where you draw directly from the pension fund, which remains invested and is known as a 'flexi-access drawdown') or via an annuity (where you receive a secure income for life.

## Drawdown

Drawdown allows you to take income directly from your pension fund without the need to purchase a lifetime annuity. In turn, this allows your pension fund to remain invested in the assets of your choice whilst taking an income.

Income drawdown is a way of using your pension pot to provide you with a regular retirement income by reinvesting it in funds specifically designed and managed for this purpose. The income you receive will vary depending on the fund's performance – it isn't guaranteed for life.

You can normally choose to take up to 25% (a quarter) of your pension pot as a tax-free lump sum. You then move the rest into one or more funds that allow you to take an income at times to suit you.

Some people use it to take a regular income. The income you receive might be adjusted periodically depending on the performance of your investments.

**There are two main types of income drawdown products:**

• Flexi-access drawdown – introduced from April 2015, where there is no limit on how much income you can choose to take from your drawdown funds

• Capped drawdown – only available before 6 April 2015 and has limits on the income you can take out; if you are already in capped drawdown, there are new rules about tax relief on future pension savings if you exceed your income cap.

There is no upper age limit on how long you may stay in drawdown, but death benefits will change when you reach age 75 if you have not withdrawn all of your benefits by this point.

Although drawdown allows people more flexibility with their pensions, income drawdown products are complex. You should always seek professional financial advice before committing to one.

# Chapter twenty-six
## Lifetime annuity

An annuity allows you to use your pension fund to buy an income from the provider of your choice. The annuity guarantees regular payments until you die. Normally, once purchased, it cannot be altered. There are different types of annuity available in the market, and you should consider the best product to suit your circumstances.

A lifetime annuity is a type of retirement income product that you buy with some or all of your pension pot. It guarantees a regular retirement income for life. Lifetime annuity options and features vary – what is suitable for you will depend on your personal circumstances, your life expectancy and your attitude to risk. You can choose to purchase a lifetime annuity with your drawdown fund at any time.

You can normally choose to take up to 25% (a quarter) of your pension pot – or of the amount you're allocating to buy an annuity – as a tax-free lump sum. You then use the rest to buy an annuity, which will provide you with a regular income for life. This retirement income is taxed as normal income.

As a rule of thumb, the older you are when you take out an annuity, the higher the income (annuity rate) you'll get.

**There are two types of lifetime annuity to choose from:**

- Basic lifetime annuities – where you set your income in advance
- Investment-linked annuities – where your income rises and falls in line with investment performance but will never fall below a guaranteed minimum.

## BASIC LIFETIME ANNUITIES
Basic lifetime annuities offer a range of income options designed to match different personal circumstances and attitude to risk.

- Choices include one that provides an income for life for you only – a single life annuity, or one that also provides an income for life for a dependant or other nominated beneficiary after you die, called a 'joint life annuity'
- Payments to continue to a nominated beneficiary for a set number of years (for example, ten years) from the time the annuity starts in case you die unexpectedly early – called a 'guarantee period'
- 'Value protection' – less commonly used but designed to pay your nominated beneficiary the value of the pot used to buy the annuity less income already paid out when you die.

Your choices affect how much income you can receive. Where you expect to live when you retire might also affect how much income you get.

If you have a medical condition, are overweight or smoke, you might be able to get a higher income by opting for an 'enhanced' or 'impaired life' annuity.

## INVESTMENT-LINKED ANNUITIES

Investment-linked annuities also pay you an income for life, but the amount you receive can fluctuate depending on how well the underlying investments perform. If the investments do well, they offer the chance of a higher income.

It's important that you are comfortable with the risk that your income could fall if the investments don't do as well as expected. All investment-linked annuities guarantee a minimum income if the fund's performance is weak.

With investment-linked annuities, you can also opt for joint or single annuity, guarantee periods, value protection, and higher rates if you have a short life expectancy due to poor health or lifestyle.

# Chapter twenty-seven
## Annuities on death

No one likes to think about dying. But naturally, you'll want to know what would happen to your finances if you were to die. If you have a single annuity and no other features, your pension stops when you die, and different tax rules will apply depending on your age.

**If you die before age 75:**
- Any lump sum payment due from a value protected annuity will be paid tax-free
- Income from a joint annuity will be paid to your dependant or other nominated beneficiary tax-free for the rest of their life
- If you die within a guarantee period, the remaining annuity payments will pass tax- free to your nominated beneficiary, then stop when the guarantee period ends.

**If you die age 75 or over:**

- Income from a joint annuity or a continuing guarantee period will be added to your beneficiary's other income and taxed as normal
- Joint annuity payments will stop when your dependant or other beneficiary dies
- Any guarantee period payments stop when the guarantee period ends
- Any lump sum due from a value protected annuity will be added to your beneficiary's income for that year and taxed as normal.

## Shopping around for annuity

Due to the current economic climate, it has never been more important to make the correct decisions when deciding how to invest a retirement fund. If you decide an annuity is right for you, it's important to shop around. It's a one-time purchase that affects your whole retirement, and you cannot change your mind later on.

You don't have to accept the annuity that your pension provider or pension scheme offers you. You have the option to shop around to find an insurance company or pension provider who will offer you a better rate.

The Open Market Option (or 'OMO') was introduced as part of the 1975 United Kingdom Finance Act and allows someone approaching retirement to 'shop around' for a number of options to convert their pension pot into an annuity, rather than simply taking the default rate offered by their pension provider.

If you stay with your current provider, you may not get the best available terms. Rates and options vary between different providers, so it's worth comparing what they can offer you. According to Moneyfacts, by shopping around you could receive up to 40% more income.

It is particularly important to shop around:

- To find out if the annuity offered by your scheme is competitive
- If you are in poor health, as this may mean you can get a higher annuity
- If your lifestyle may qualify you for a higher annuity, for example, if you smoke or do a particular type of job.

## CONSUMERS COULD BE MISSING OUT ON THOUSANDS OF POUNDS

Research finds consumers could be missing out on thousands of pounds in retirement by not shopping around for their pension product. This means their pension pot may not stretch as far as they hope it will, yet a significant proportion of people expect their retirement income to cover much more than just the essentials.

Research conducted by the Pensions Policy Institute for LV= has found that in 2016, there were around 30,000 people who took out an annuity with their existing provider and missed out on additional income by not shopping around. In total, they lost out on an additional £130 million, which equates to on average £4,000 over the course of their retirement.

## MISSING OUT ON A BOOST TO YOUR RETIREMENT INCOME

Since April 2015, you've been able to withdraw as much of the money as you want when you reach age 55, although it will be taxed as income. Arranging an annuity is a complicated process, so it's important to know what you need to do at each stage. And it's vital that you shop around to get the best annuity rate, as you could miss out on a boost to your income if you fail to do so.

The research also identified that people are increasingly expecting their retirement income to cover more than just the essentials, which means their money needs to work even harder. Nearly six in ten (57%) of those planning to retire in the next five years want their retirement income to also cover home maintenance costs, while 53% want it to cover holidays and a quarter (24%) say they'd like to leave money behind as an inheritance. In addition, one in six (17%) want to be able to use their retirement income to help their children or grandchildren with a property purchase, and 14% would like care costs to be covered as well.

## PROFESSIONAL FINANCIAL ADVICE

Taking professional financial advice is the best way for someone to ensure their retirement savings meet all their needs throughout retirement. While some people may not understand the need for advice, the value of it is clear to consumers who have used it. Nearly nine in ten (87%) of those who took advice feel confident they made the right choice about what to do with their money, while three quarters (75%) say financial advice helped get more for their money. Revealingly, one in five (19%) who didn't take financial advice say that even though they don't regret not using it now, they worry that they might regret it in the future.

Last year alone, consumers missed out on a staggering £130 million over their retirement by remaining with the same provider when taking out an annuity. This is echoed across the retirement space, with consumers failing to access the best retirement products. People are expecting their pension pot to stretch even further nowadays, so it's crucial they take control and get support to help them make the most of their savings.

*Source data:*
*Methodology for consumer survey: Opinium, on behalf of LV=, conducted online interviews with 2,404 UK adults between 12 and 27 March 2017. Data has been weighted to reflect a nationally representative audience.*
*Methodology for amount missed out on in retirement: the Pensions Policy Institute (PPI) reported that around 80,000 annuities are purchased each year, of which 52% are purchased from the existing provider. PPI calculated that if 80% of those who purchased an annuity from their existing provider continue to lose around 6.8% of retirement income, that could represent a loss of around £130 million over the lifetimes of those purchasing in annuities in 2016.*
*[1] LV= calculated that 52% of 80,000 annuities were taken out each year with existing providers, 80% of which would lose out on retirement income, equating to 30,000 people. With 30,000 people missing out on £130 million, that works out at around £4,000 per person throughout retirement.*

# Chapter twenty-eight
## Self-invested personal pension benefits on death

If you die, your Self-Invested Personal Pension benefits will be paid to your beneficiaries – either as a lump sum or an ongoing pension. You'll need to complete a nomination form declaring who you want the payments to go to. The tax treatment of any death benefits paid from your SIPP will depend on your circumstances.

**IF YOU DIE BEFORE THE AGE OF 75**
Upon receipt of a death certificate, the investments held under your SIPP will be realised and their full cash value used to provide benefits for your spouse or registered civil partner, dependants, family members, or other beneficiaries nominated by you for this purpose.

The scheme trustees will decide who will receive benefits and the form of the benefits, in their absolute discretion. However, they will take into account any wishes you would have expressed through the completion of a death benefit expression of wish. You may complete a new nomination at any time.

A beneficiary can usually elect to receive their benefit as a lump sum or a flexi-access dependant's pension. Alternatively, they may be able to use it to purchase a dependant's annuity with an insurance company of their choosing.

Payments of death benefits are normally free of any Income Tax or Inheritance Tax, but there is no guarantee that this will be the case. Any amount of the fund over your personal lifetime allowance may be subject to a tax charge, which will be determined by your personal representatives. If a beneficiary dies whilst still in receipt of the death benefits you bequeathed them, then the remaining benefits will be paid to a successor.

The successor or successors will be selected by the scheme trustees in their absolute discretion and can be anyone appointed by the beneficiary or selected by the scheme trustees in light of the beneficiary's personal circumstances.

### IF YOU DIE AFTER AGE 75
If you die after age 75, then the process is the same as described above. A tax charge will be levied upon payment of the benefits, however.

Payments will be taxed in accordance with PAYE based on the recipient's marginal rate. If you do not leave a surviving spouse, registered civil partner or dependants, then the value of your fund may be paid to a charity nominated by you for this purpose. Any funds paid to a charity will be exempt from tax.

If you die after the age of 75, any subsequent payment of death benefits are not subject to the lifetime allowance.

# Chapter twenty-nine
## Pensions and Divorce

**IMPORTANCE OF TAKING PENSIONS INTO ACCOUNT**

Pensions vary in complexity. Some are relatively straightforward whilst others, in particular public sector or other final salary schemes, can be much more complicated. When a marriage breaks down, a couple might not appreciate the importance of taking pensions into account as a key asset – and perhaps even the most valuable asset – on divorce. It may be that you're a long way from retirement, and how you're going to manage then may not seem the most pressing issue. However, it's important not to underestimate or overlook pensions and consider how this could eventually impact on your retirement.

The courts have long had the power to take pensions into account in dividing up the matrimonial assets. Over the years, you may have paid into a number of workplace and personal pension schemes, as well as the additional State Pension. You'll need to obtain a valuation for each one. This will be based on what your pension would be worth if you moved it elsewhere. Typically, the total will be below the current fund value because any charges or penalties for transferring out of the scheme will be included. If you live in England, Northern Ireland or Wales, you will need to obtain a statement that gives you the cash equivalent transfer value. If you live in Scotland, your pension value will be based on what was paid in after you married or entered into a civil partnership, up to the date of separation.

## HOW YOU DIVIDE THEM BETWEEN YOU
Once you've obtained the value of all your pensions, you need to think about how you will divide them between you. It is important to realise that there is no automatic entitlement to pension sharing. People often seem to think that just because they have been married, they are entitled to half of everything – including the pension. That is not the case. Divorce pension entitlement is more subtle than that.

When disputes arise within families, emotions run high and rash decisions can be made. This is why divorce is an arena fraught with acrimony. But seven in ten couples don't consider pensions during divorce proceedings, leaving some women short-changed by £5 billion [1] every year. Research shows that more than half of married people (56%) would fight for a fair share of any jointly owned property, and 36% would want to split their combined savings.

## WOMEN ARE LESS WELL PREPARED FOR RETIREMENT
Fewer than one in ten (9%) claim they want a fair share of pensions, despite the average married couple's retirement pot totaling £132k – that's more than five times the average UK salary (£26k) [2]. In fact, more married people would be concerned about losing a pet during a settlement than sharing a pension (13% vs 9%).

Overall, women are less well prepared for retirement than men, with 52% saving adequately for the future compared with 59% respectively. This figure falls to below half (49%) for divorced women, with nearly a quarter (24%) saying they are unable to save anything at all into a pension – twice the rate of divorced men (12%) saving nothing. Furthermore, two fifths of divorced women (40%) say their retirement prospects became worse as a result of the split, compared with just 19% of men.

Even if pensions are discussed during a divorce settlement, women are still missing out – 16% lost access to any pension pot when they split with their partner, and 10% were left relying completely on the State Pension.

## WHAT HAPPENS TO PENSIONS WHEN A COUPLE GETS DIVORCED?

Almost half of women (48%) have no idea what happens to pensions when a couple gets divorced, which may explain why so few couples consider them as part of a settlement. A fifth (22%) presume each partner keeps their own pension, and 15% believe they are split 50/50, no matter what the circumstances. In reality, pensions can be dealt with in a number of ways on divorce.

## PENSION SHARING

Divorce courts can and often do order a pension to be shared when considering financial arrangements during a divorce. Other options however include offsetting which is where the pension fund value is 'offset' against other matrimonial assets, such as the house. To offset a pension or part of a pension against another capital asset has to be done carefully because of the different nature of capital assets and pensions. Pension are not liquid assets; they can only be turned into cash at retirement.

When a pension is divided or shared, this does not mean that you will receive a cash lump sum – although in certain circumstances where the recipient is over retirement age, that can be the case. A pension or part of a pension that is ordered from one party to another still remains a pension and has to be invested in a pension plan.

## PENSION OFFSETTING

The value of the pension is weighed against another asset, such as the family home. If you choose this option, your ex could be awarded a larger share of the property in return for you keeping your pension. However, they will have to make their own retirement arrangements. If they're close to retirement and haven't made any pension arrangements of their own, they may not agree to offsetting.

## PENSION EARMARKING

Pension earmarking means one of you receives a lump sum or income from the other person's pension when they start to draw on it. However, the pension holder may decide not to take their pension straight away or carry on working, leaving the other person without a retirement income. If you're dependent on pension earmarking and you remarry, you will lose your right to carry on receiving the pension – and if your ex dies, your income is likely to stop.

## DEFERRED LUMP SUM

You receive a lump sum when the pension holder retires. This option is not available in Scotland.

## DEFERRED PENSION SHARING

If your ex is below the age at which they can receive a pension and you are already receiving one, you can ask the court to make a Deferred Pension Sharing Order. This allows you to receive an unreduced pension until they reach the age at which they can start to receive a pension too. This option is not available in Scotland.

If you're retired, you can still split pensions if your ex has already retired, but it won't be possible for a tax-free lump sum to be taken from their pension – even if they took a lump sum.

[1] The research was carried out online for Scottish Widows by YouGov across a total of 5,314 nationally representative adults in April 2017. Additional research was carried out by Opinium across a total of 5,000 nationally representative adults in September 2017.[2] ONS Earnings and working hours
www.ons.gov.uk/employmentandlabourmarket/peopleinwork/earningsandworkinghours
[3] Based on Ministry of Justice figures showing there were 11,503 'pension sharing orders' in the year to March 2017, and ONS data that shows there were 107,071 divorces in 2016.

# **Chapter thirty**
## Protecting yourself from scams

Fraudsters are getting more deceitful and ever more successful. Pension and investment scams are on the increase in the UK. Everyday fraudsters are using sophisticated ways to part savers from their money, and the Internet and advances in digital communications mean these kinds of scams are getting more common and harder to identify. A lifetime's savings can be lost in moments.

Nearly one in ten over-55s fear they have been targeted by suspected scammers since the launch of pension freedoms, new research [1] shows.

## Tactics commonly used to defraud

The study found 9% of over-55s say they have been approached about their pension funds by people they now believe to be scammers since the rules came into effect from April 2015. Offers to unlock or transfer funds are tactics commonly used to defraud people of their retirement savings.

One in three (33%) over-55s say the risk of being defrauded of their savings is a major concern following pension freedoms. However, nearly half (49%) of those approached say they did not report their concerns because they did not know how to or were unaware of who they could report the scammers to.

## Reporting suspected scammers to authorities

Most recent pension fraud data[2] from ActionFraud, the national fraud and cybercrime reporting service, shows 991 cases have been reported since the launch of pension freedoms involving losses of more than £22.687 million

## Alternative investments such as wine offered

The research found fewer than one in five (18%) of those approached by suspected scammers had reported their fears to authorities. Nearly half (47%) said the approaches involved offers to unlock pension funds or access money early, and 44% said they involved transferring pensions.

About 28% of those targeted by suspected fraudsters were offered alternative investments such as wine, and 20% say they were offered overseas investments, while 13% say scammers had suggested investing in crypto currencies. Around 6% believe they have been victims of fraud.

## Safeguarding hard-earned retirement savings

Pension freedoms, though enormously popular with consumers, have created a potentially lucrative opportunity for fraudsters, and people need to be vigilant to safeguard their hard-earned retirement savings.

If it sounds too good to be true, then it usually is, and people should be sceptical of investments that are offering unusually high rates of return or which invest in unorthodox products which may be difficult to understand. If in any doubt, seeking professional financial advice from a regulated adviser will help ensure you don't get caught out.

Source data:
The Financial Services Compensation Scheme.

**Some scammers have very convincing websites and other online presence, which make them look like a legitimate company. Always check with the FCA to make sure they're registered**

## Top five financial scams to look out for in the UK

### 1. Boiler-room schemes
These scams promise investors impressive returns, but they deliver nothing apart from a great big loss. More than 5,000 investors lost a combined £1.73 billion through boiler-room schemes reported to the Action Fraud crime-prevention centre in 2014. Victims will receive a telephone call out of the blue and be offered an investment opportunity with sky-high returns of as much as 40%. You will most likely be told that you must act fast and asked to transfer your money straight away. It's common for victims to part with tens of thousands of pounds. Boiler rooms are not authorised by the Financial Conduct Authority (FCA). This means that if you hand over your cash, it might be the last you will see of it.

### Take Action
Check the FCA status of any firm you intend to deal with for investments. Call 0800 1116768 or go to www.fca.org.uk/register.

### 2. Phishing/smishing
The most common scams come from fraudsters posing as someone official, such as your bank or building society. Typically, you receive an email or text asking you to click a link and verify login, account and password details. The communication received is from a fraudster who will be able to read the information you type in, should you fall for their trick. This information is then used to raid your account. If you lose money this way, you won't get it back.

## Take Action
Your bank will never ask you to disclose full security and password details, so alarm bells should ring. If in doubt, call your bank and ask them if they have tried to contact you.

## 3. Pension liberation
Scammers are bombarding people aged 55 and over with bogus investment opportunities to try to get hold of their pension savings.
One of the most common scams since the pension freedoms were announced involves alleged investment opportunities abroad
Low interest rates are tempting some people to take extra risks, so they are vulnerable to such fake investments. Fraudsters can approach you by post, email or telephone.

## Take Action
If you're offered a 'must-have' investment or a free pension 'review' out of the blue, be wary. Also, be concerned if you're warned that the deal is limited and you must act now. Choosing the right retirement income product is a big decision and shouldn't be done quickly or under pressure.

Consult a registered professional financial adviser. If you think that you may have been made a fraudulent offer, contact Action Fraud on 0300 1232040 or visit the FCA's Scam  Smart site to see if the investment you've  been offered is on their warning list:
http://scamsmart.fca.org.uk/warninglist.

## 4. Homebuying fraud
This con intercepts cash transferred as a home deposit to a solicitor in the lead-up to exchange and completion. It's all done via the Internet where a computer hacker monitors emails sent between a solicitor and client. When a bank transfer is about to be made, the fraudster emails the homebuyer pretending to be the solicitor, telling them the details of the law firm's bank account have changed. The unsuspecting homebuyer sends their cash to the new account, where it is withdrawn by the fraudsters.

## Take Action

If you're buying a property, watch for any emails about payments, such as a change in bank details at the last minute. Many victims are told that the account is being 'audited', and so another one must be used. Ring your solicitor if you're in any doubt.

## 5. Freebie scams

Seemingly free trial offers for products are duping consumers out of millions of pounds a year. To get the freebies, you need to enter your card details – although told you won't be charged for the introductory period. In fact, you are often signing up to an expensive monthly subscription that is very difficult to get out of. Once this type of billing is approved – known as 'continuous payment authorisation' – up to £100 a month can be taken without any further contact.

## Take Action

Report such free trial offers to The Advertising Standards Authority contact 020 7492 2222 or to make a complaint visit https://www.asa.org. uk/make-a-complaint.html

INFORMATION PROVIDED AND ANY OPINIONS EXPRESSED ARE FOR GENERAL GUIDANCE ONLY AND NOT PERSONAL TO YOUR CIRCUMSTANCES OR ARE INTENDED TO PROVIDE SPECIFIC ADVICE. PROFESSIONAL FINANCIAL ADVICE SHOULD BE OBTAINED. WE ACCEPT NO RESPONSIBILITY FOR ANY LOSS ARISING TO ANY PERSON FROM ACTION AS A RESULT OF THIS GUIDE.

PROVIDING OPPORTUNITIES FOR THE FUTURE

# The Foundation provides local financial resources in the form of gifts to youth clubs, schools and organisations.

We fund structured, purposeful projects and ventures in and around Shropshire and Cheshire, giving youths the opportunity of reaching their full potential.

## Work we have supported for the community

We have supported many projects that have positively impacted many groups of people within the community we have donated to date over £25,000 to:

Team funding, Sports equipment and kits, Charity fundraising activities, School projects, Guides, Scouts and Youth Clubs.

Please donate now and help us continue with our good work...

Every pound you put in is a pound that is given out.

All running costs are covered.

# Glossary of Financial Terms

### A

*Alpha*

Alpha is a measure of a fund's over or under performance compared to its benchmark. It represents the return of the fund when the benchmark is assumed to have a return of zero. It shows the extra value that the manager's activities seem to have contributed. If the Alpha is 5, the fund has outperformed its benchmark by 5% and the greater the Alpha, the greater the out performance.

*Alternative Assets*

Includes private real estate, public real estate, venture capital, non-venture private equity, hedge funds, distressed securities, oil and gas partnerships, event arbitrage, general arbitrage, managed funds, commodities, timber and other.

*American Stock Exchange*

AMEX is the second-largest stock exchange in the U.S., after the New York Stock Exchange (NYSE). In general, the listing rules are a little more lenient than those of the NYSE, and thus the AMEX has a larger representation of stocks and bonds issued by smaller companies than the NYSE. Some index options and interest rate options trading also occurs on the AMEX. The AMEX started as an alternative to the NYSE. It originated when brokers began meeting on the curb outside the NYSE in order to trade stocks that failed to meet the Big Board's stringent listing requirements, but the AMEX now has its own trading floor. In 1998, the parent company of the NASDAQ purchased the AMEX and combined their markets, although the two continue to operate separately. Also called The Curb.

*Annual Rate of Return*

There are several ways of calculating this. The most commonly used methodologies reflect the compounding effect of each period's increase or decrease from the previous period.

*Annual Percentage Rate (APR)*

The APR is designed to measure the "true cost of a loan". The aim is to create a level playing field for lenders preventing them from advertising a low rate and hiding fees. In the case of a mortgage the APR should reflect the yearly cost of a mortgage, including interest, mortgage insurance, and the origination fee, expressed as a percentage.

*Annual Premium Equivalent*

Calculated as regular premiums plus 10% of single premiums.

*Arbitrage*

A financial transaction or strategy that seeks to profit from a price differential perceived with respect to related or correlated instruments in different markets. Typically involves the simultaneous purchase of an instrument in one market and the sale of the same or related instrument in another market.

*Asset Allocation*

Apportioning of investment funds among categories of assets such as cash equivalents, stock, fixed-income investments, alternative investments such as hedge funds and managed futures funds, and tangible assets like real estate, precious metals and collectibles.

*Average Monthly Gain*

The average of all the profitable months of the fund.

*Average Monthly Loss*

The average of all the negative months of the fund.

*Average Monthly Return*

The average of all the monthly performance numbers of the fund.

# B

## Basis Point
A basis point is one one-hundredth of a percent i.e. 50 basis points or "bps" is 0.5%.

## Bear / Bear Market
Bear is a term describing an investor who thinks that a market will decline. The term also refers to a short position held by a market maker. A Bear Market is a market where prices are falling over an extended period.

## Bellwether
A stock or bond that is widely believed to be an indicator of the overall market's condition. Also known as Barometer stock.

## Beta
Beta is a measure of a fund's volatility compared to its benchmark, or how sensitive it is to market movements. A fund with a Beta close to 1 means that the fund will move generally in line with the benchmark.  Higher than 1 and the fund is more volatile than the benchmark, so that with a Beta of 1.5, say, the fund will be expected to rise or fall 1.5 points for every 1 point of benchmark movement. If this Beta is an advantage in a rising market – a 15% gain for every 10% rise in the benchmark –the reverse is true when markets fall. This is when managers will look for Betas below 1, so that in a down market the fund will not perform as badly as its benchmark.

## Bid Price
The price at which an investor may sell units of a fund back to the fund manager. It is also the price at which a market maker will buy shares.

## Blue Chips
Large, continuously well performing stock, presumed to be among the safer investments on an exchange.

*Bond*

A debt investment, with which the investor loans money to an entity (company or Government) that borrows the funds for a defined period of time at a specified interest rate. The indebted entity issues investors a certificate, or bond, that states the interest rate (coupon rate) that will be paid and when the loaned funds are to be returned (maturity date). Interest on bonds is usually paid every six-months.

*Bond Rating Codes*

| Rating | S&P | Moody's |
|---|---|---|
| Highest quality | AAA | Aaa |
| High quality | AA | Aa |
| Upper medium quality | A | A |
| Medium grade | BBB | Baa |
| Somewhat speculative | BB | Ba |
| Low grade, speculative | B | B |
| Low grade, default possible | CCC | Caa |
| Low grade, partial recovery possible | CC | Ca |
| Default, recovery unlikely | C | C |

*Bottom up Investing*

An approach to investing which seeks to identify well performing individual securities before considering the impact of economic trends.

*BRIC*

A term used to refer to the combination of Brazil, Russia, India and China. General consensus is that the term was first prominently used in a thesis of the Goldman Sachs Investment Bank. The main point of this 2003 paper was to argue that the economies of the BRICs are rapidly developing and by the year 2050 will eclipse most of the current richest countries of the world. Due to the popularity of the Goldman Sachs thesis, "BRIC" and "BRIMC" (M for Mexico), these terms are also extended to "BRICS" (S for South Africa) and "BRICKET" (including Eastern Europe and Turkey) and have become more generic terms to refer to these emerging markets.

*Bull / Bull Market*

An investor who believes that the market is likely to rise. A Bull Market is a market where prices are rising over an extended period.

*Bulldog Bond*

A sterling denominated bond that is issued in London by a company that is not British. These sterling bonds are referred to as bulldog bonds as the bulldog is a national symbol of England.

# C

*Child Trust Fund*

A Child Trust Fund is a savings and investment account for children. Children born on or after 1st September 2002 will receive a £250 voucher to start their account. The account belongs to the child and can't be touched until they turn 18, so that children have some money behind them to start their adult life. Payments or contributions can be made up to a maximum of £1,200 per 12-month period (starting on the birthday of the child), excluding the voucher amount. Interest and capital growth will be earned tax-free. Additional deposits can be made by parents, grandparents or anyone else.

*Closed-end Fund*

Type of fund that has a fixed number of shares or units. Unlike open-ended mutual funds, closed-end funds do not stand ready to issue and redeem shares on a continuous basis.

*Collar*

A contract that protects the holder from a rise or fall in interest rates or some other underlying security above or below certain fixed points. The contract offers the investor protection from interest rate moves outside of an expected range.

*Constant Proportion Portfolio Insurance CPPI*

Strategy that basically buys shares as they rise and sells shares as they fall. To implement a CPPI strategy, the investor selects a floor below which the portfolio value is not allowed to fall. The floor increases in value at the rate of return on cash. If you think of the difference between the assets and floor as a "cushion", then the

CPPI decision rule is to simply keep the exposure to shares a constant multiple of the cushion.

*Consumer Discretionary Sector*

The array of businesses included in the Consumer Discretionary Sector are categorized into five industry groups. They are: Automobiles and Components; Consumer Durables and Apparel; Hotels, Restaurants and Leisure; Media; and Retailing.

*Consumer Staples*

The industries that manufacture and sell food/beverages, tobacco, prescription drugs and household products. Proctor and Gamble would be considered a consumer staple company because many of its products are household and food related.

*Convertible Arbitrage*

This is an investment strategy that involves taking a long position on a convertible security and a short position in its converting common stock. This strategy attempts to exploit profits when there is a pricing error made in the conversion factor of the convertible security.

*Convertible Bond*

A bond that can be exchanged, at the option of the holder, for a specific number of shares of the company's preferred stock or common stock. Convertibility affects the performance of the bond in certain ways. First and foremost, convertible bonds tend to have lower interest rates than nonconvertible's because they also accrue value as the price of the underlying stock rises. In this way, convertible bonds offer some of the benefits of both stocks and bonds. Convertibles earn interest even when the stock is trading down or sideways, but when the stock prices rise, the value of the convertible increases. Therefore, convertibles can offer protection against a decline in stock price. Because they are sold at a premium over the price of the stock, convertibles should be expected to earn that premium back in the first three or four years after purchase.

## Core Fund

Fund that takes a middle of the road approach to generate returns for shareholders. These funds are generally structured in two ways. One strategy is to combine stocks and bonds (and possible income trusts) into a single fund to achieve a steady return and improved asset allocation. The other approach is to combine growth stocks and value stocks to diversify the risk from the typical ups and downs of markets. This type of fund can also be called a blend fund since it can show characteristics of a pure growth fund or a pure value fund. Either way, a core fund is focused to producing long-term results.

## Corporate Bonds

Corporate Bonds are similar to gilts but are a form of borrowing by companies rather than Governments. Let's say Astra Zeneca wished to borrow a billion pounds for research and development. They would initially approach their brokers who would review the strength of Astra Zeneca versus the Government to assess what is a reasonable "risk premium". A secure company might be able to borrow money at 1 or 2 percentage points above the gilt rate and a very insecure company may have to pay 10 percentage points above the Government rate or in some cases substantially more. Companies' security is generally graded from AAA to no rating, the less secure debt being known in the UK as "High Yield", or as it is more accurately described by Americans as "Junk Bonds". So with Corporate Bonds the short term returns will vary in line with interest rates as they do with gilts, but also in line with the perceived strength of the company.

## Correlation

A standardised measure of the relative movement between two variables, such as the price of a fund and an index. The degree of correlation between two variables is measured on a scale of −1 to +1. If two variables move up or down together, they are positively correlated. If they tend to move in opposite directions, they are negatively correlated.

*Coupon*
Denotes the rate of interest on a fixed interest security. A 10 % coupon pays interest of 10 % a year on the nominal value of the stock.

*Cyclical Stock*
The stock of a company which is sensitive to business cycles and whose performance is strongly tied to the overall economy. Cyclical companies tend to make products or provide services that are in lower demand during downturns in the economy and higher demand during upswings. Examples include the automobile, steel, and housing industries. The stock price of a cyclical company will often rise just before an economic upturn begins and fall just before a downturn begins. Investors in cyclical stocks try to make the largest gains by buying the stock at the bottom of a business cycle, just before a turnaround begins. Opposite of defensive stock.

## D

*Debenture*
A loan raised by a company, paying a fixed rate of interest and secured on the assets of the company.

*Defensive Stock*
A stock that tends to remain stable under difficult economic conditions. Defensive stocks include food, tobacco, oil, and utilities. These stocks hold up in hard times because demand does not decrease as dramatically as it may in other sectors. Defensive stocks tend to lag behind the rest of the market during economic expansion because demand does not increase as dramatically in an upswing.

*Delta*
The rate at which the price of an option changes in response to a move in the price of the underlying security. If an option's delta is 0.5 (out of a maximum of 1), a $2 move in the price of the underlying will produce a $1 move in the option.

*Delta Hedge*
A hedging position that causes a portfolio to be delta neutral.

*Derivatives*
Financial contracts whose value is tied to an underlying asset. Derivatives include futures and options.

*Discount*
When a security is selling below its normal market price, opposite of premium.

*Distressed Securities*
A distressed security is a security of a company which is currently in default, bankruptcy, financial distress or a turnaround situation.

# E

*Efficient Frontier*
A line created from the risk-reward graph, comprised of optimal portfolios. The optimal portfolios plotted along the curve have the highest expected return possible for the given amount of risk.

*EFTA – European Fair-Trade Association*
A network of 11 Fair Trade organisations in nine European countries which import Fair Trade products from some 400 economically disadvantaged producer groups in Africa, Asia and Latin America. EFTA's members are based in Austria, Belgium, France, Germany, Italy, the Netherlands, Spain, Switzerland and the United Kingdom.

*Embedded Value EV*
A method of accounting used by life insurance business. The embedded value is the sum of the net assets of the insurance business under conventional accounting and the present value of the in-force business based on estimates of future cash flows and conservative assumptions about for example, mortality, persistence and expenses. Accounts users prefer this method because it gives a separate indication of new business profitability, a key performance indicator for a life insurer.

*Emerging Markets*
Typically includes markets within countries that have an underdeveloped or developing infrastructure with significant potential for economic growth and increased capital market participation for foreign investors. These countries generally possess some of the following characteristics; per capita GNP less than $9000, recent economic liberalisation, debt ratings below investment grade, recent liberalisation of the political system and non membership of the Organisation of Economic Cooperation and Development. Because many emerging countries do not allow short selling or offer viable futures or other derivatives products with which to hedge, emerging market investing entails investing in geographic regions that have underdeveloped capital markets and exhibit high growth rates and high rates of inflation. Investing in emerging markets can be very volatile and may also involve currency risk, political risk and liquidity risk. Generally, a long-only investment strategy.

*Emerging Markets Debt*
Debt instruments of emerging market countries. Most bonds are US Dollar denominated and a majority of secondary market trading is in Brady bonds.

*Equities*
Ownership positions in companies that can be traded in public markets. Often produce current income which is paid in the form of quarterly dividends. In the event of the company going bankrupt equity holders' claims are subordinate to the claims of preferred stockholders and bondholders.

*Equity Hedge*
Also known as long / short equity, combines core long holdings of equities with short sales of stock or stock index options. Equity hedge portfolios may be anywhere from net long to net short depending on market conditions. Equity hedge managers generally increase net long exposure in bull markets and decrease net long exposure or are even net short in a bear market.

## Equity Market Neutral

This investment strategy is designed to exploit equity market inefficiencies and usually involves being simultaneously long and short equity portfolios of the same size within a country. Market neutral portfolios are designed to be either beta or currency neutral or both. Attempts are often made to control industry, sector and market capitalisation exposures.

## Equity Risk

The risk of owning stock or having some other form of ownership interest.

## Ethical Investing

Choosing to invest in companies that operate ethically, provide social benefits, and are sensitive to the environment. Also called socially conscious investing.

## EU

European Union. The economic association of over a dozen European countries which seek to create a unified, barrier-free market for products and services throughout the continent. The majority of countries share a common currency with a unified authority over that currency. Notable exceptions to the common currency are the UK, Sweden, Norway, Denmark.

## Eurobond

A bond issued and traded outside the country whose currency it is denominated in, and outside the regulations of a single country; usually a bond issued by a non-European company for sale in Europe. Interest is paid gross.

## Eurozone or Euroland

The collective group of countries which use the Euro as their common currency.

## Event Driven Investing

Investment strategy seeking to identify and exploit pricing inefficiencies that have been caused by some sort of corporate event such as a merger, spin-off, distressed situation or recapitalisation.

*Exit Fee*

A fee paid to redeem an investment. It is a charge levied for cashing in a fund's capital.

*Exposure*

The condition of being subjected to a source of risk.


## F


*FCP*

Fonds Commun de Placement. FCPs are a common fund structure in Luxembourg. In contrast to SICAV, they are not companies, but are organised as co-ownerships and must be managed by a fund management company.

*Feeder Fund*

A fund which invests only in another fund. The feeder fund may be a different currency to the main fund and may be used to channel cash in to the main fund for a different currency class.

*Fixed Interest*

The term fixed interest is often used by banks and building societies relating to an account that pays a set rate of interest for a set time period. This type of investment is capital secure and the returns are known at outset. However, fixed interest within the investment world is a completely different concept. It is used to describe funds that invest in Government Gilts and Corporate Bond securities.

*Fixed Income Arbitrage*

Investment strategy that seeks to exploit pricing inefficiencies in fixed income securities and their derivative instruments. Typical investment is long a fixed income security or related instrument that is perceived to be undervalued and short a similar related fixed income security or related instrument. Often highly leveraged.

*Floating Rate*

Any interest rate that changes on a periodic basis. The change is usually tied to movement of an outside indicator, such as the Bank of England Base Rate. Movement above or below certain levels is often prevented by a predetermined floor and ceiling for a given rate. For example, you might see a rate set at "base plus 2%". This means that the rate on the loan will always be 2% higher than the base rate, which changes regularly to take into account changes in the inflation rate. For an individual taking out a loan when rates are low, a fixed rate loan would allow him or her to "lock in" the low rates and not be concerned with fluctuations. On the other hand, if interest rates were historically high at the time of the loan, he or she would benefit from a floating rate loan, because as the prime rate fell to historically normal levels, the rate on the loan would decrease. Also called adjustable rate.

*Floor*
    A contract that protects the holder against a decline in interest rates or prices below a certain point.

*Forward*
    An agreement to execute a transaction at some time in the future. In the foreign exchange market this is a tailor-made deal where an investor agrees to buy or sell an amount of currency at a given date.

*Forward Rate Agreement (FRA)*
    A type of forward contract that is linked to interest rates.

*FTSE 100*
    The Financial Times Stock Exchange 100 stock index, a market cap weighted index of stocks traded on the London Stock Exchange. Similar to the S&P 500 in the United States.

*Fund of Funds*
    An investment vehicle that invests in more than one fund. Portfolio will typically diversify across a variety of investment managers, investment strategies and subcategories. Provides investors with access to managers with higher minimums than individuals might otherwise afford.

*Funds under Management*
Total amount of funds managed by an entity, excluding

## G

*Gearing*
The effect that borrowing has on the equity capital of a company or the asset value of a fund. If the assets bought with funds borrowed appreciate in value, the excess of value over funds borrowed will accrue to the shareholder, thus augmenting, or gearing up the value of their investment.

*Geographic Spread*
The distribution in a fund's portfolio over different parts of the world, either by countries or larger areas.

*Gilt-Edged Securities*
Stocks and shares issued and guaranteed by the British government to raise funds and traded on the Stock Exchange. A relatively risk-free investment, gilts bear fixed interest and are usually redeemable on a specified date. The term is now used generally to describe securities of the highest value. According to the redemption date, gilts are described as short (up to five years), medium, or long (15 years or more).

*Gilts*
Gilts are effectively Government borrowing. When the Chancellor does not have sufficient income to meet his expenditure, then the Government will often borrow money in the form of gilts. These can be for a variety of different terms, paying a range of interest                                                                  rates.

A typical example would be a ten-year gilt which may pay, say, 5% income. This is the most secure investment you could buy, as you know the rate of return and you know when you will receive your capital back. The UK Government has never defaulted on a gilt.

If however you wanted to access your money before maturity then you would have to sell your gilt on the open market. Let's say you were trying to sell your gilt after one year. In order to obtain a value any potential purchaser will look at the term remaining on your gilt and the interest rate promised and compare this to new gilts being launched at the time. If the Government was then launching a new gilt over a nine-year time period, and promising to pay 6% per annum, then clearly nobody is going to want to pay the same amount of money for your gilt which is offering a lower interest rate.

They would probably therefore offer at least 9% less than you originally paid for it to reflect the 1% difference in income over the nine years of the remaining term. So, whilst you had set out to achieve guaranteed returns, if you sell a gilt before maturity you could potentially make a capital loss on it, in this instance a loss of 9% over the year.

However, if you decide to keep the gilt until its maturity you will still receive all of your interest and the capital back. Having said this, your valuation each year will vary depending on market conditions.

*GNMA (Ginnie Mae)*
Government National Mortgage Association. A U.S. Government-owned agency which buys mortgages from lending institutions, securitizes them, and then sells them to investors. Because the payments to investors are guaranteed by the full faith and credit of the U.S. Government, they return slightly less interest than other mortgage-backed securities.

*Growth Stocks*
Stock of a company which is growing earnings and/or revenue faster than its industry or the overall market. Such companies usually pay little or no dividends, preferring to use the income instead to finance further expansion.

*Growth Orientated Portfolios*
Dominant theme is growth in revenues, earnings and market share. Many of these portfolios are hedged to mitigate against declines in the overall market.

*Global Macro*
The investment strategy is based on shifts in global economies. Derivatives are often used to speculate on currency and interest rate movements.

*Guided Architecture*
In relation to funds, for example FPIL Premier policyholders may only go into the FPIL mirror fund range – this is guided architecture. In contrast to FPIL Reserve policyholders who may choose any security – open architecture.


## H

*Hawk*
An investor who has a negative view towards inflation and its effects on markets. Hawkish investors prefer higher interest rates in order to maintain reduced inflation.

*Hedge*
Any transaction with the objective of limiting exposure to risk such as changes in exchange rates or prices.

*Hedge Fund*
A pooled investment vehicle that is privately organised, administered by investment management professionals and generally not widely available to the general public. Many hedge funds share a number of characteristics; they hold long and short positions, use leverage to enhance returns, pay performance or incentive fees to their managers, have high minimum investment requirements and target absolute returns. Generally, hedge funds are not constrained by legal limitations on their investment discretion and can adopt a variety of trading strategies. The hedge fund manager often has its own capital (or that of its principals) invested in the hedge fund it manages.

*Herding*
Hedge fund managers while taking a position may encourage other investors to follow this trend.

### High Conviction Stock Picking

A typical portfolio is not constrained by benchmarks, allowing the manager to pursue an approach where a smaller number of stocks are chosen that may bear little or no resemblance to the consensus view. i.e the manager's conviction.

### High Water Mark

The assurance that a fund only takes fees on profits actually earned by an individual investment. For example, a £10 million investment is made in year one and the fund declines by 50%, leaving £5 million in the fund. In year two, the fund returns 100% bringing the investment value back to £10 million. If a fund has a high water mark it will not take incentive fees on the return in year two since the investment has never grown. The fund will only take incentive fees if the investment grows above the initial level of £10 million.

### High-Yield Bond

Often called junk bonds, these are low grade fixed income securities of companies that show significant upside potential. The bond has to pay a high yield due to significant credit risk.

### Hurdle Rate

The minimum investment return a fund must exceed before a performance-based incentive fee can be taken. For example if a fund has a hurdle rate of 10% and the fund returned 18% for the year, the fund will only take incentive fees on the 8 percentage points above the hurdle rate.

### I

### Index

An arithmetic mean of selected stocks intended to represent the behaviour of the market or some component of it. One example is the FTSE 100 which adds the current prices of the one hundred FTSE 100 stocks and divides the results by a pre-determined number, the divisor.

## Index Funds

A fund that attempts to achieve a performance similar to that stated in an index. The purpose of this fund is to realise an investment return at least equal to the broad market covered by the indices while reducing management costs.

## Index Linked Gilt

A gilt, the interest and capital of which change in line with the Retail Price Index.

## In the Money

A condition where an option has a positive intrinsic value.

## Intrinsic Value

A component of the market value of an option. If the strike price of a call option is cheaper than the prevailing market price, then the option has a positive intrinsic value, and is "in the money".

## Investment Grade

Something classified as investment grade is, by implication, medium to high quality.

1) In the case of a stock, a firm that has a strong balance sheet, considerable capitalization, and is recognized as a leader in its industry.
2) In the case of fixed income, a bond with a rating of BBB Or higher.

## J

## January Effect

Tendency of US stock markets to rise between December 31 and the end of the first week in January. The January Effect occurs because many investors choose to sell some of their stock right before the end of the year in order to claim a capital loss for tax purposes. Once the tax calendar rolls over to a new year on January 1st these same investors quickly reinvest their money in the market, causing stock prices to rise. Although the January Effect has been observed numerous times throughout history, it is difficult for investors to profit from it since the market as a whole expects it to happen and therefore adjusts its prices accordingly.

*Junk Bond*
A bond that pays a high yield due to significant credit risk

*L*

*Leverage*
When investors borrow funds to increase the amount they have invested in a particular position, they use leverage. Sometimes managers use leverage to enable them to put on new positions without having to take off other positions prematurely. Managers who target very small price discrepancies or spreads will often use leverage to magnify the returns from these discrepancies. Leverage both magnifies the risk of the strategy as well as creates risk by giving the lender power over the disposition of the investment portfolio. This may occur in the form of increased margin requirements or adverse market shifts, forcing a partial or complete liquidation of the portfolio.

The amount of leverage used by the fund is commonly expressed as a percentage of the fund. For example if the fund has £1 million and borrows another £2 million to bring the total invested to £3 million, then the fund is leveraged 200%

*Life Cycle Funds*
Life-cycle funds are the closest thing the industry has to a maintenance-free retirement fund. Life-cycle funds, also referred to as "age-based funds" or "target-date funds", are a special breed of the balanced fund. They are a type of fund of funds structured between equity and fixed income. But the distinguishing feature of the life-cycle fund is that its overall asset allocation automatically adjusts to become more conservative as your expected retirement date approaches. While life-cycle funds have been around for a while, they have been gaining popularity.

*LIBOR*
London Inter Bank Offered Rate.

*Liquidity*
1) The degree to which an asset or security can be bought or sold in the market without affecting the asset's price. Liquidity is characterized by a high level of trading activity.
2) The ability to convert an asset to cash quickly.
Investing in illiquid assets is riskier because there might not be a way for you to get your money out of the investment. Examples of assets with good liquidity include blue chip common stock and those assets in the money market. A fund with good liquidity would be characterised by having enough units outstanding to allow large transactions without a substantial change in price.

*Liquidity Risk*
Risk from a lack of liquidity, ie an investor having difficulty getting their money out of an investment.

*Listed Security*
Stock or bond that has been accepted for trading by an organised and registered securities exchange. Advantages of being listed are an orderly market place, more liquidity, fair price determination, accurate and continuous reporting on sales and quotations, information on listed companies and strict regulations for the protection of securities holders.

*Lock Up / Lock In*
Time period during which an initial investment cannot be redeemed.

*Long Position*
Holding a positive amount of an asset (or an asset underlying a derivative instrument)

*Long / Short Hedged*
Also described as the Jones Model. Manager buys securities he believes will go up in price and sells short securities he believes will decline in price. Manager will be either net long or net short and may change the net position frequently. For example, a manager may be 60% long and 100% short, giving him a market exposure of 40% net short. The basic belief behind this strategy is that it will enhance the

manager's stock picking ability and protect investors in all market conditions.

*M*

*Macro-Economics*
The field of economics that studies the behaviour of the economy as a whole. Macroeconomics looks at economy-wide phenomena such as changes in unemployment, national income, rate of growth, and price levels.

*Managed Accounts*
Accounts of individual investors which are managed individually by an investment manager. The minimum size is usually in excess of £3 million.

*Managed Futures*
An approach to fund management that uses positions in government securities, futures contracts, options on futures contracts and foreign exchange in a portfolio. Some managers specialise in physical commodity futures but most find they must trade a variety of financial and non-financial contracts if they have considerable assets under management.

*Management Fee*
The fees taken by the manager on the entire asset level of the investment. For example, if at the end of the period the investment is valued at £1 million and the management fee is 1.2%, then the fee would be £12,000.

*Margin*
The amount of assets that must be deposited in a margin account in order to secure a portion of a party's obligations under a contract. For example, to buy or sell an exchange traded futures contract, a party must post a specified amount that is determined by the exchange, referred to as initial margin. In addition, a party will be required to post variation margin if the futures contracts change in value. Margin is also required in connection with the purchase and

sale of securities where the full purchase price is not paid up front or the securities sold are not owned by the seller.

## Market Maker
An Exchange member firm that is obliged to make a continuous two-way price, that is to offer to buy and sell securities in which it is registered throughout the mandatory quote period.

## Market Neutral Investing
An investment strategy that aims to produce almost the same profit regardless of market circumstances, often by taking a combination of long and short positions. This approach relies on the manager's ability to make money through relative valuation analysis, rather than through market direction forecasting. The strategy attempts to eliminate market risk and be profitable in any market condition.

## Market Risk
Risk from changes in market prices

## Market Timing
1) An accepted practice of allocating assets among investments by switching into investments that appear to be beginning an up trend and switching out of investments that appear to be starting a downtrend.
2) An increasingly unacceptable / illegal practice of undertaking frequent or large transactions in mutual funds. Especially where there is a time difference between the close of the relevant markets that the fund invests in and the valuation of the fund. ie a Far East fund that is valued the next day in the UK.

## Market Value
The value at which an asset trades or would trade in the market.

## Mark to Market
When the value of securities in a portfolio are updated to reflect the changes that have occurred due to the movement of the underlying market. The security will then be valued at its current market price.

## Maximum Draw Down

The largest loss suffered by a security or fund, peak to trough, over a given period, usually one month.

## Merger Arbitrage

Sometimes called Risk Arbitrage, involves investment in event-driven situations such as leveraged buy outs, mergers and hostile takeovers. Normally the stock of an acquisition target appreciates while the acquiring company's stock decreases in value.

## Mezzanine Level

Stage of a company's development just prior to its going public. Venture capitalists entering at that point have a lower risk of loss than at previous stages and can look forward to early capital appreciation as a result of the market value gained by an initial public offering.

## Micro-Economics

The behaviour and purchasing decisions of individuals and firms.

## Money Market Funds

Mutual funds that invest in short term highly liquid money market instruments. These funds are used when preservation of capital is paramount. They may be used to "park" money between investments, especially during periods of market uncertainty.

## Mortgage Backed Security

A pass-through security that aggregates a pool of mortgage-backed debt obligations. Mortgage-backed securities' principal amounts are usually government guaranteed. Homeowners' principal and interest payments pass from the originating bank through a government agency or investment bank, to investors, net of a loan servicing fee payable to the originator.

*Multi-Manager Product*

An investment pool that allocates assets to a number of managers with different investment styles. This methodology facilitates a high degree of diversification and accordingly the potential for a greater spread of risk. Hedge funds often have this structure. Smaller investors are able to enjoy access to a greater variety of managers that would normally be prohibited by minimum investment requirements for each manager. Funds of funds are a classic multi-manager product.

*Municipal Bond (USA)*

A debt security issued by a state, municipality, or county, in order to finance its capital expenditures. Municipal bonds are exempt from federal taxes and from most state and local taxes, especially if you live in the state the bond is issued. Such expenditures might include the construction of highways, bridges or schools. "Munis" are bought for their favourable tax implications and are popular with people
in high income tax brackets.

*Mutual Fund*

A security that gives small investors access to a well diversified portfolio of equities, bonds, and other securities. Each shareholder participates in the gain or loss of the fund. Shares are issued and can be redeemed as needed. The fund's net asset value (NAV) is determined each day. Each mutual fund portfolio is invested to match the objective stated in the prospectus. Some examples of mutual funds are UK Unit Trusts, Open-ended

Investment Companies (OEICs), EU registered UCITS, Lūzembourg based SICAVs.

**N**

*NAREIT*

National Association of Real Estate Investment Trusts

*Nasdaq*

A computerised system established by the NASD to facilitate trading by providing broker/dealers with current bid and ask price quotes on over-the-counter stocks and some listed stocks. Unlike the Amex and the NYSE, the Nasdaq (once an acronym for the National Association of securities Dealers Automated Quotation system) does not have a physical trading floor that brings together buyers and sellers. Instead, all trading on the Nasdaq exchange is done over a network of computers and telephones. Also, the Nasdaq does not employ market specialists to buy unfilled orders like the NYSE does. The Nasdaq began when brokers started informally trading via telephone; the network was later formalized and linked by computer in the early 1970s. In 1998 the parent company of the Nasdaq purchased the Amex, although the two continue to operate separately. Orders for stock are sent out electronically on the Nasdaq, where market makers list their buy and sell prices. Once a price is agreed upon, the transaction is executed electronically.

*Net Asset Value (NAV)*

NAV equals the closing market value of all assets within a portfolio after subtracting all liabilities including accrued fees and expenses. NAV per share is the NAV divided by the number of shares in issue. This is often used as the price of a fund. A purchase fee may be added to the NAV when buying units in the fund. This fee is typically 1-7%.

*Net Exposure*

The exposure level of a fund to the market. It is calculated by subtracting the short percentage from the long percentage. For example, if a fund is 100% long and 30% short, then the net exposure is 70% long.

*Nominee Name*

Name in which a security is registered and held in trust on behalf of the beneficial owner.

# O

*Offer Price*
The price at which a fund manager or market maker will sell shares to you. (ie offer them to you). The offer price is higher than the Bid Price which is the price at which they will buy shares from you. (ie they will make a bid). This is one way in which a market maker turns a profit. A fund manager may use the difference to cover dealing administration costs.

*Offshore*
Located or based outside of one's national boundaries. Typically, these locations have preferential tax treatments and fund legislation.

*Open Architecture*
In relation to funds, for example FPIL Reserve policyholders may choose any security – open architecture. In contrast to FPIL Premier policyholders who may only go into the FPIL mirror fund range – this is guided architecture.

*Open-ended Funds*
These are funds where units or shares can be bought and sold daily and where the number of units or shares in issue can vary daily.

*Opportunistic Investing*
A general term describing any fund that is opportunistic in nature. These types of funds are usually aggressive and seek to make money in the most efficient way at any given time. Investment themes are dominated by events that are seen as special situations or short-term opportunities to capitalise from price fluctuations or imbalances, such as initial public offering.

*Option*
A privilege sold by one party to another that offers the buyer the right, but not the obligation, to buy (call)or sell (put) a security at an agreed-upon price during a certain period of time or on a specific date. Options are extremely versatile securities that can be used in many different ways. Traders use options to speculate, which is a

relatively risky practice, while hedgers use options to reduce the risk of holding an asset.

*Over the Counter- OTC*

A security traded in some context other than on a formal exchange such as the LSE, NYSE, DJIA, TSX, AMEX, etc. A stock is traded over the counter usually because the company is small and unable to meet listing requirements of the exchanges. Also known as unlisted stock, these securities are traded by brokers/dealers who negotiate directly with one another over computer networks and by phone. The Nasdaq, however, is also considered to be an OTC market, with the tier 1 being represented by companies such as Microsoft, Dell and Intel. Instruments such as bonds do not trade on a formal exchange and are thus considered over-the- counter securities. Most debt instruments are traded by investment banks making markets for specific issues. If someone wants to buy or sell a bond, they call the bank that makes the market in that bond and ask for quotes. Many derivative instruments such as forwards, swaps and most exotic derivatives are also traded OTC.

*Out of the Money*

This refers to options:
1) For a call, when an option's strike price is higher than the market price of the underlying stock.
2) For a put, when the strike price is below the market price of the underlying stock.
Basically, an option that would be worthless if it expired today.

*Over-Hedging*

Locking in a price, such as through a futures contract, for more goods, commodities or securities that is required to protect a position. While hedging does protect a position, over-hedging can be costly in the form of missed opportunities. Although you can lock in a selling price, over-hedging might result in a producer or seller missing out on favourable market prices. For example, if you entered into a January futures contract to sell 25,000 shares of 'Smith Holdings' at $6.50 per share you would not be able to take advantage if the spot price jumped to $7.00.

*Overlay Strategy*

A type of derivatives strategy. This strategy is often employed to provide protection from currencies or interest rate movements that are not the primary focus of the main portfolio strategy.

*Overweight*

Refers to an investment position that is larger than the generally accepted benchmark. For example, if a company normally holds a portfolio whose weighting of cash is 10%, and then increases cash holdings to 15%, the portfolio would have an overweight position in cash.

## P

*Pair Trading*

The strategy of matching a long position with a short position in two stocks of the same sector. This creates a hedge against the sector and the overall market that the two stocks are in. The hedge created is essentially a bet that you are placing on the two stocks; the stock you are long in versus the stock you are short in. It's the ultimate strategy for stock pickers, because stock picking is all that counts. What the actual market does won't matter (much). If the market or the sector moves in one direction or the other, the gain on the long stock is offset by a loss on the short.

*Percent Long*

The percentage of a fund invested in long positions.

*Percent Short*

The percentage of a fund that is sold short.

*Performance Fee*

The fee payable to the fund adviser on new profits earned by the fund for the period.

*Portfolio Turnover*

The number of times an average portfolio security is replaced during an accounting period, usually a year.

*Premium*

The total cost of an option. The premium of an option is basically the sum of the option's intrinsic and time value. It is important to note that volatility also affects the premium.

The difference between the higher price paid for a fixed-income security and the security's face amount at issue. If a fixed-income security (bond) is purchased at a premium, existing interest rates are lower than the coupon rate. Investors pay a premium for an investment that will return an amount greater than existing interest rates.

*Price Earnings Ratio (P/E Ratio)*

A valuation ratio of a company's current share price compared to its per-share earnings. Calculated as: Market Value per Share/Earnings per Share (EPS)

EPS is usually from the last four quarters (trailing P/E), but sometimes can be taken from the estimates of earnings expected in the next four quarters (projected or forward P/E). A third variation is the sum of the last two actual quarters and the estimates of the next two quarters.

Sometimes the P/E is referred to as the "multiple," because it shows how much investors are willing to pay per dollar of earnings. In general, a high P/E means high projected earnings in the future. However, the P/E ratio actually doesn't tell us a whole lot by itself. It's usually only useful to compare the P/E ratios of companies in the same industry, or to the market in general, or against the company's own historical P/E.

*Prime Broker*

A broker which acts as settlement agent, provides custody for assets, provides financing for leverage, and prepares daily account statements for its clients, who might be money managers, hedge funds, market makers, arbitrageurs, specialists and other professional investors.

*Private Placement / Private Equity*

When equity capital is made available to companies or investors, but not quoted on a stock market. The funds raised through private equity can be used to develop new products and technologies, to expand working capital, to make acquisitions, or to strengthen a company's balance sheet. The average individual investor will not have access to private equity because it requires a very large investment. The result is the sale of securities to a relatively small number of investors. Private placements do not have to be registered with organizations such as the FSA, SEC because no public offering is involved.

*Proprietary Trading*

When a firm trades for direct gain instead of commission dollars. Essentially, the firm has decided to profit from the market rather than commissions from processing trades. Firms who engage in proprietary trading believe they have a competitive advantage that will enable them to earn excess returns.

*Prospectus*

In the case of mutual funds, a prospectus describes the fund's objectives, history, manager background, and financial statements. A prospectus makes investors aware of the risks of an investment and in most jurisdictions is required to be published by law.

*Protected Cell Company*

A standard limited company that has been separated into legally distinct portions or cells. The revenue streams, assets and liabilities of each cell are kept separate from all other cells. Each cell has its own separate portion of the PCC's overall share capital, allowing shareholders to maintain sole ownership of an entire cell while owning only a small proportion of the PCC as a whole. PCCs can provide a means of entry into a captive insurance market to entities for which it was previously uneconomic. The overheads of a protected cell captive can be shared between the owners of each of the cells, making the captive cheaper to run from the point of view of the insured.

*Purification*

The process whereby Muslims give to charity any interest deemed to have been credited to their holdings in funds or stocks.

*Put Option*

An option giving the holder the right, but not the obligation, to sell a specific quantity of an asset for a fixed price during a specific period.

**Q**

*Qualitative Analysis*

Analysis that uses subjective judgment in evaluating securities based on non-financial information such as management expertise, cyclicality of industry, strength of research and development, and labour relations.

*Quantitative Analysis*

A security analysis that uses financial information derived from company annual reports and income statements to evaluate an investment decision. Some examples are financial ratios, the cost of capital, asset valuation, and sales and earnings trends.

*Quasi Sovereign Bond*

Debt issued by a public sector entity that is, like a sovereign bond, guaranteed by the sovereign, however there is a difference in that there may be a timing difference in repayment in the unlikely event of default.

**R**

*REIT Real Estate Investment Trust*

A security that trades like a stock on the major exchanges and invests in real estate directly, through either properties or mortgages.

REITs receive special tax considerations and typically offer investors high yields, as well as a highly liquid method of investing in real estate. Equity REITs invest in and own properties (thus responsible for the equity or value of their real estate assets). Their revenues come principally from their properties' rents. Mortgage REITs deal in investment and ownership of property mortgages. These REITs loan money for mortgages to owners of real estate or purchase existing mortgages or mortgage-backed securities. Their revenues are generated primarily by the interest that they earn on the mortgage loans. Hybrid REITs combine the investment strategies of equity REITs and mortgage REITs by investing in both properties and mortgages.

## R – Squared
A statistical measure that represents the percentage of a fund's or security's movements that are explained by movements in a benchmark index. It is a measure of correlation with the benchmark. R-squared values range from 0 to 100. An R-squared of 100 means that all movements of a security are completely explained by movements in the index. ie perfect correlation.

## Repurchase Agreement (Repo)
A form of short-term borrowing for dealers in government securities. The dealer sells the government securities to investors, usually on an overnight basis, and buys them back the following day. For the party selling the security (and agreeing to repurchase it in the future) it is a repo; for the party on the other end of the transaction (buying the security and agreeing to sell in the future) it is a reverse repurchase agreement. Repos are classified as a money-market instrument. They are usually used to raise short-term capital.

## Risk Adjusted Rate of Return
A measure of how much risk a fund or portfolio took on to earn its returns, usually expressed as a number or a rating. This is often represented by the Sharpe Ratio. The more return per unit of risk, the better

## Risk Arbitrage
A broad definition for three types of arbitrage that contain an element of risk:

1) Merger and Acquisition Arbitrage - The simultaneous purchase of stock in a company being acquired and the sale (or short sale) of stock in the acquiring company.

2) Liquidation Arbitrage - The exploitation of a difference between a company's current value and its estimated liquidation value.

3) Pairs Trading - The exploitation of a difference between two very similar companies in the same industry that have historically been highly correlated. When the two company's values diverge to a historically high level you can take an offsetting position in each (e.g. go long in one and short the other) because, as history has shown, they will inevitably come to be similarly valued.

In theory true arbitrage is riskless, however, the world in which we operate offers very few of these opportunities. Despite these forms of arbitrage being somewhat risky, they are still relatively low-risk trading strategies which money managers (mainly hedge fund managers) and retail investors alike can employ.

## Risk-Free Rate

The quoted rate on an asset that has virtually no risk. The rate quoted for US treasury bills are widely used as the risk-free rate.

## Risk Reward Ratio

This is closely related to the Sharpe Ratio, except the risk reward ratio does not use a risk-free rate in its calculation. The higher the risk reward ratio, the better. Calculated as: Annualised rate of return/Annualised Standard Deviation

# S

## Santa Claus Rally

The rise in US stock prices that sometimes occurs in the week after Christmas, often in anticipation of the January effect.

## Satellite Fund

Specialist mandate fund that offers greater breadth of proposition than a "core" fund.

## Secondary Market

A market in which an investor purchases an asset from another investor, rather than an issuing corporation. A good example is the London Stock Exchange. All stock exchanges are part of the secondary market, as investors buy securities from other investors instead of an issuing company.

## Sector Fund

A mutual fund whose objective is to invest in a particular industry or sector of the economy to capitalise on returns. Because most of the stocks in this type of fund are all in the same industry, there is a lack of diversification. The fund tends to do very well or not well at all, depending on the conditions of the specific sector.

## Securities

General name for all stocks and shares of all types.

## Securities Lending

When a brokerage lends securities owned by its clients to short sellers. This allows brokers to create additional revenue (commissions) on the short sale transaction.

## Semi-gilt

A financial instrument through which a municipality or parastatal (owned or controlled wholly or partly by the government) borrows money from the public in exchange for a fixed repayment plan.

## SICAV

SICAV stands for Societe D'Investissement a Capital Variable. It is a Luxembourg incorporated company that is responsible for the management of a mutual fund and manages a portfolio of securities. The share capital is equal to the net assets of the fund. The units in the portfolio are delivered as shares and the investors are referred to as shareholders. SICAVs are common fund structures in Luxembourg.

## Sharia(h)

Sharia refers to the body of Islamic law. The term means "way" or "path"; it is the legal framework within which public and some private aspects of life are regulated for those living in a legal system based on Muslim principles.

*Sharpe Ratio*
A ratio developed by Bill Sharpe to measure risk-adjusted performance. It is calculated by subtracting the risk-free rate from the rate of return for a portfolio and dividing the result by the standard deviation of the portfolio returns.

Calculated as: Expected Portfolio Return – Risk Free Rate/Portfolio Standard Deviation

The Sharpe ratio tells us whether the returns of a portfolio are because of smart investment decisions or a result of excess risk. The Sortino Ratio is a variation of this.

*Short Selling*
The selling of a security that the seller does not own, or any sale that is completed by the delivery of a security borrowed by the seller. Short sellers assume that they will be able to buy the stock at a lower amount than the price at which they sold short. Selling short is the opposite of going long. That is, short sellers make money if the stock goes down in price. This is an advanced trading strategy with many unique risks and pitfalls.

*Small Caps*
Stocks or funds with smaller capitalisation. They tend to be less liquid than blue chips, but they tend to have higher returns.

*Soft Commissions*
A means of paying brokerage firms for their services through commission revenue, as opposed to normal payments. For example, a mutual fund may offer to pay for the research of a brokerage firm by executing trades at the brokerage.

*Sovereign Debt*
A debt instrument guaranteed by a government.

*Special Situations Investing*

Strategy that seeks to profit from pricing discrepancies resulting from corporate event transactions such as mergers and acquisitions, spin-offs, bankruptcies or recapitalisations. Type of event-driven strategy.

*Specific Risk*

Risk that affects a very small number of assets. This is sometimes referred to as "unsystematic risk." An example would be news that is specific to either one stock or a small number of stocks, such as a sudden strike by the employees of a company you have shares in or a new governmental regulation affecting a particular group of companies. Unlike systematic risk or market risk, specific risk can be diversified away.

*Spin Off*

A new, independent company created through selling or distributing new shares for an existing part of another company. Spinoffs may be done through a rights offering.

*Sponsors*

Lead investors in a fund who supply the seed money. Often the general partner in a hedge fund.

*Spread*

1) The difference between the bid and the offer prices of a security or asset.

2) An options position established by purchasing one option and selling another option of the same class, but of a different series

*Standard Deviation*

Tells us how much the return on the fund is deviating from the expected normal returns.

### Stop-Loss Order

An order placed with a broker to sell a security when it reaches a certain price. It is designed to limit an investor's loss on a security position. This is sometimes called a "stop market order." In other words, setting a stop-loss order for 10% below the price you paid for the stock would limit your loss to 10%.

### Strategic Bond Funds

Invest primarily in higher yielding assets including high yield bonds, investment grade bonds, preference shares and other bonds. The funds take strategic asset allocation decisions between countries, asset classes, sectors and credit ratings.

### Strike Price

The stated price per share for which underlying stock may be purchased (for a call) or sold (for a put) by the option holder upon exercise of the option contract.

### Swap

Traditionally, the exchange of one security for another to change the maturity (bonds), quality of issues (stocks or bonds), or because investment objectives have changed. Recently, swaps have grown to include currency swaps and interest rates swaps. If firms in separate countries have comparative advantages on interest rates, then a swap could benefit both firms. For example, one firm may have a lower fixed interest rate, while another has access to a lower floating interest rate. These firms could swap to take advantage of the lower rates.

### Swaption (Swap Option)

The option to enter into an interest rate swap. In exchange for an option premium, the buyer gains the right but not the obligation to enter into a specified swap agreement with the issuer on a specified future date.

### Swing Trading (Swings)

A style of trading that attempts to capture gains in a stock within one to four days. To find situations in which a stock has this extraordinary potential to move in such a short time frame, the trader must act quickly. This is mainly used by at-home and day traders. Large institutions trade in sizes too big to move in and out of stocks quickly. The individual trader is able to exploit the short-term stock movements without the competition of major traders. Swing traders use technical analysis to look for stocks with short-term price momentum. These traders aren't interested in the fundamental or intrinsic value of stocks but rather in their price trends and patterns.

*Systematic Risk*

The risk inherent to the entire market or entire market segment. Also known as "un-diversifiable risk" or "market risk." interest rates, recession and wars all represent sources of systematic risk because they will affect the entire market and cannot be avoided through diversification. Whereas this type of risk affects a broad range of securities, unsystematic risk affects a very specific group of securities or an individual security. Systematic risk can be mitigated only by being hedged.

*Systemic Risk*

Risk that threatens an entire financial system.

*S&P500*

Standard & Poor's Index of the New York Stock Exchange. A basket of 500 stocks that are considered to be widely held. The S&P 500 index is weighted by market value, and its performance is thought to be representative of the stock market as a whole.

*T*

*Treasury Bill*

A negotiable debt obligation issued by the U.S. government and backed by its full faith and credit, having a maturity of one year or less. Exempt from state and local taxes. Also called Bill or T-Bill or U.S. Treasury Bill.

*Time Value*

The amount by which an option's premium exceeds its intrinsic value. Also called time premium.

## Top-Down Investing

An investment strategy which first finds the best sectors or industries to invest in, and then searches for the best companies within those sectors or industries. This investing strategy begins with a look at the overall economic picture and then narrows it down to sectors, industries and companies that are expected to perform well. Analysis of the fundamentals of a given security is the final step.

## Tracking Error

This statistic measures the standard deviation of a fund's excess returns over the returns of an index or benchmark portfolio. As such, it can be an indication of 'riskiness' in the manager's investment style. A Tracking Error below 2 suggests a passive approach, with a close fit between the fund and its benchmark. At 3 and above the correlation is progressively looser: the manager will be deploying a more active investment style and taking bigger positions away from the benchmark's composition.

## Traded Endowment Policy - TEP

An Endowment Policy is a type of life insurance that has a value that is payable to the insured if he/she is still living on the policy's maturity date, or to a beneficiary otherwise. They are normally "with profits policies". If the insured does not wish to wait until maturity to receive the value, they can either surrender it back to the issuing insurance company, or they can sell the policy on the open market. If the policy is sold it then becomes a Traded Endowment Policy or TEP. TEP Funds aim to buy and sell TEPs at advantageous prices to make a profit.

## Traded Options

Transferable options with the right to buy or sell a standardised amount of a security at a fixed price within a specified period.

## Traditional Investments

Includes equities, bonds, high yield bonds, emerging markets debt, cash, cash equivalents.

# U

## Umbrella Fund

An investment company which has a group of sub-funds (pools) each having its own investment portfolio. The purpose of this structure is to provide investment flexibility and widen investor choice.

## Underlier or Underlying Security

A security or commodity, which is subject to delivery upon exercise of an option contract or convertible security. Exceptions include index options and futures, which cannot be delivered and are therefore settled in cash.

## Underweight

A situation where a portfolio does not hold a sufficient amount of securities to satisfy the accepted benchmark of the portfolio's asset allocation strategy. For example, if a portfolio normally holds 40% stock and currently holds 30%, the position in equities would be considered underweight.

## Unit Trust

A common form of collective investment (similar to a mutual fund) where investors' money is pooled and invested into a variety of shares and bonds in order to reduce risk. Its capital structure is open ended as units can be created or redeemed depending on demand from investors. It should be noted that a Unit Trust means something completely different in the US.

# V

## Value of New Business VNB

Sum of all income (i.e. charges) from new policies minus costs of setting up the policies (i.e. commission) discounted to present day value.

## Value Stocks

Stocks which are perceived to be selling at a discount to their intrinsic or potential worth, i.e. undervalued; or stocks which are out of favour with the market and are under-followed by analysts. It is believed that the share price of these stocks will increase as the value of the company is recognised by the market.

*Value-Added Monthly Index (VAMI)*
An index that tracks the monthly performance of a hypothetical $1000 investment. The calculation for the current month's VAMI is: Previous VAMI x (1 + Current Rate of Return)

The value-added monthly index charts the total return gained by an investor from reinvestment of any dividends and additional interest gained through compounding. The VAMI index is sometimes used to evaluate the performance of a fund manager.

*Venture Capital*
Money and resources made available to start-up firms and small businesses with exceptional growth potential. Venture capital often also includes managerial and technical expertise. Most venture capital money comes from an organized group of wealthy investors who seek substantially above average returns and who are willing to accept correspondingly high risks. This form of raising capital is increasingly popular among new companies that, because of a limited operating history, can't raise money through a debt issue. The downside for entrepreneurs is that venture capitalists usually receive a say in the major decisions of the company in addition to a portion of the equity.

*Volatility*
Standard deviation is a statistical measurement which, when applied to an investment fund, expresses its volatility, or risk. It shows how widely a range of returns varied from the fund's average return over a particular period. Low volatility reduces the risk of buying into an investment in the upper range of its deviation cycle, then seeing its value head towards the lower extreme. For example, if a fund had an average return of 5%, and its volatility was 15, this would mean that the range of its returns over the period had swung between +20% and -10%. Another fund with the same average

return and 5% volatility would return between 10% and nothing, but there would at least be no loss.

Printed in Great Britain
by Amazon